Kirtley Library
Columbia College
8th and Rogers
Columbia, MO. 65201

CHRISTIAN EDUCATION/PUBLIC SCHOOLS

CHRISTIAN EDUCATION/PUBLIC SCHOOLS

A Teacher's Interpretation

ELIZABETH M. MACHEN

With a Foreword by A. Joe Poole

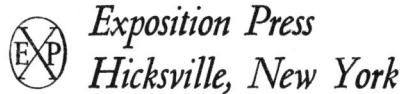

Exposition Press
Hicksville, New York

FIRST EDITION

© 1978 by Elizabeth M. Machen

All rights reserved, including the right of reproduction in whole or in part, in any form or by any means, electronic or mechanical, including photocopying, recording, or by any information storage and retrieval system. No part of this book may be reproduced without permission in writing from the publisher. Inquiries should be addressed to Exposition Press, Inc., 900 South Oyster Bay Road, Hicksville, N.Y. 11801

ISBN 0-682-48990-5

Printed in the United States of America

To all pedagogical students who "joy" in the task of increasing "in wisdom and stature, and in favour with God and man."

CONTENTS

	Foreword	9
One	MASTER	13
Two	LET US REASON TOGETHER	18
Three	BEING IN THE WAY	24
Four	IF YE LOVE ME	29
Five	RENDER TO CAESAR	33
Six	LORD, TEACH US TO PRAY	37
Seven	ASK, SEEK, FIND	42
Eight	LEARN OF ME	49
Nine	SPARE THE ROD	54
Ten	BE YE PERFECT	59
Eleven	YE SHALL RECEIVE POWER	63
Twelve	GO YE . . .	73
Thirteen	IF MY PEOPLE	79
Fourteen	FOR TEN'S SAKE	84
Fifteen	THE COUNSEL OF THE UNGODLY	88
Sixteen	RIVERS OF LIVING WATER	92

FOREWORD

Working as a Chaplain, I have been involved in both the hospital and industrial settings for the past ten years. A major area of concern to me is the growing number of people with no spiritual resources upon which to draw in their problems of everyday living.

It seems to me the church is missing the great masses of people in the area of religious instructions and training. Consequently, the home of our current society is 'missing the mark' (αμαρτια New Testament Gk:SIN) in the moral, ethical, religious, and spiritual training of children and youth.

While being a member of a denomination which has stood for complete separation of Church and State, I have some reservations as to just how far this is practical and even possible. History has proved the dangers of a church dominated society, but who can deny the religious and spiritual motives of many of our ancestors and forefathers as they settled and populated this continent.

To deprive our children the privilege and blessings (happiness) of the spiritual aspects of life is to cripple them to a point where they, and in turn society as we know it can no longer survive.

The author of this book has been a dedicated teacher for over sixteen years. She is a devoted Christian with a searching mind and has given much thought to this important and relevant subject. It is my hope and prayer that all concerned with the public and private aspects of education will give careful and thoughtful attention to the information contained within.

—A. JOE POOLE
Lumberton, North Carolina
August 1, 1976

CHRISTIAN EDUCATION/PUBLIC SCHOOLS

ONE

MASTER

The answers to any educational persuasion should be sought in the Scriptures, for this claim is given in II Timothy 3:16,17: "All scripture is given by inspiration of God, and is profitable for doctrine, for reproof, for correction, for instruction in righteousness: That the man of God may be perfect, throughly furnished unto all good works."

Familiar to most of us, the First and Fourteenth Amendments to our Constitution forbid Congress or any other branch of the government from regulating any law " . . . respecting an establishment of religion, or prohibiting the free exercise thereof. . . ." As understood, the Supreme Court interprets this meaning as protection of the people from governmental involvement in their religion or their churches, and prohibits individuals or churches to use public funds to achieve religious purposes or to use the power of government to force beliefs or worship on anyone.

This seems to be in agreement with the Scriptures, for in our pluralistic nation of almost every denominational and nondenominational group, as in His day, Jesus did not force His prayer life, worship, or scriptural studies on anyone. He lived and spoke this witness into being among His faithful. "They received the word with all readiness of mind and searched the scriptures daily, whether those things were so." (ACTS: 17:11.) "But Paul increased the more in strength, and confounded the Jews . . . proving that this is very Christ." (ACTS 9:22.)

The several modern translations available in our classroom

library, along with a broad selection of other resources, give varied choices of interpretations of our students' consideration in their research of the world's great literature. In our social studies collection, we may use The King James Bible, The Douay Version, The Book of Mormon, The Koran, and any others that are obtainable and are relevant. Atheism is included for it is legally listed by our government as a religion. Here the pace is set for a study of truths. Continual searching helps to establish the facts. No, we are not teaching any particular religion, but we are providing a laboratory for honest research, of secular subjects.

Some of our sixth graders have scored reading ability levels at tenth grade plus. In our one-room school house setting, we strive to satisfy every inquisition. Each year's turnout seems to produce more knowledgeable young adults, because of the responsibilities and demands of modern times. Our Current Events-News Broadcast discussions bring forth their maturity. Yes, it is written of Jesus when he was at this wonderful age of twelve, that he " . . . increased in wisdom and stature, and in favour with God and man." (LUKE 2:52.)

As these kaleidoscopic glimpses into classroom procedures are given, attention may be focused on claiming my own legal rights and responsibilities as a citizen of the United States to exercise Christian educational principles in a public school classroom without violating constitutional rulings. A study of secular educational principles reveals a correlation with the educational principles exemplified by Jesus Christ.

"And there are also many other things which Jesus did, the which, if they should be written every one, I suppose that even the world itself could not contain the books that should be written. Amen." (JOHN 21:25.)

Some background explanations of my personal convictions are in order here: The majestic love of God, our Heavenly Father, who created the total Heavens and Earth, and saw that this was good. His plan for creation man was intimate, for He yearned to personally fellowship with us, to speak audibly, to guide us constantly and directly into His presence eternally. Yet early in the Old Testament account, man's iniquities began to separate him from his King and Creator.

As a student in Old and New Testament Religion at Furman University, Greenville, S.C., I was grieved to realize that man in Old Testament times reduced God's accessibility to a small Holy of Holies compartment, with a high priest only as mediator. Rejoicing came with Malachi's accurate forecast of a new covenant to mankind as another miracle.

Life's tribulations were real to me as a teenager. Even more real were the joys, the hopes, and excitements of a wonderful journey into Heaven accompanied personally by a Lord God who loved us, and who loves us " . . . the same yesterday, and to day, and for ever." (HEBREWS 13:8.)

This master of masters, a glorious triune God, in His great love, set an example for our desperations. To fulfill His promise of claiming us to Himself, He became flesh and dwelt among us as our Way, our Truth, and our Life. (JOHN 14:6.)

A blueprint was given to us, a map to follow in His Holy Scriptures, and a personal guide—the Holy Spirit. Oh, the glorious wealth of our Heavenly Father who is mighty to be praised!

We are not our own for we had absolutely nothing to do with our birth into His marvelous creation. He even bought us with a price—this mysterious "blood atonement." This great sacrifice of the love of Jesus Christ, who was obedient unto death that we might live eternally with Him in glory and in praise to Him forever—even now.

Basic educational principles, as any student of the Scriptures realizes, were established by God and were exercised by Jesus during His earthly ministry, and now by the Holy Spirit. "I am the Lord thy God, which teacheth thee to profit, which leadeth thee by the way thou shouldest go." (ISAIAH 48:17.)

Jesus was the existing embodiment of truth. He was, with His Father, the great "I AM." (EXODUS 3:14, JOHN 10:30.) The Scriptures indicate that His divine and human qualifications as a teacher were inherent and developed. As the only perfect human being who has lived or ever will live on this earth, He invites us to learn of Him. (MATTHEW 11:29.) "Let this mind be in you, which was also in Christ Jesus" (PHILIPPIANS 2:5.)

Creativity and originality were in the beginning with God. Man has only to discover what our Lord created, and to invent what our Lord God originated. (COLOSSIANS 1:16.)

In every possible way of existence, our Lord has experienced before us, living more completely than man can experience, and suffering more than we could ever bear. Such is our example to follow in every phase of our being.

Directly from the Scriptures are the profound traits of our example teacher. "He taught them as one that had authority, and not as the scribes." (MARK 1:22.)

The individuality of the Master Teacher amazes any student. With His divine nature: "He himself knew what was in man." (JOHN 2:52.) He had all knowledge—the depth of understanding of our human nature. Beyond our ability he knew even the very thoughts of the people. He personally sought out the individual to reveal his needs, abilities, thoughts and purposes, and to help this learner to become fulfilled in body, mind, and spirit as a total person, a completed creation in eternal perspective.

He was also the Master of teaching methods. Because of His individualized approaches, His variety of techniques will always be under constant surveillance: questioning sessions, conversations, discourses, discussions, lectures, revelations, stories, art, audio-visual aids, dramatics, demonstrations, gesticulations, projects, continuities, examples, involvements, strategies, clarifications, aims and objectives, cause and effect, previews and reviews, meanings and scopes, examinations, repetitions, conversions, regenerations, transformations.

Jesus' approaches were exacting. His demonstrations were clearly defined, and His culminations were thoroughly made. He was and is the Master Teacher.

" . . . It is expedient for you that I go away: for if I go not away, the Comforter will not come unto you; but if I depart, I will send him unto you. And when he is come, he will reprove the world of sin, and of righteousness, and of judgment: Of sin, because they believe not in me; Of righteousness, because I go to my Father, and ye see me no more; Of judgment, because the prince of this world is judged. . . . When he, the Spirit of truth, is come, he will guide you into all truth: for he shall not speak of himself; but whatsoever he shall hear, that shall he speak: and he will shew you things to come. He shall glorify me: for he shall receive of mine, and shall shew it unto you." (JOHN 16:7-14.)

TWO

LET US
REASON TOGETHER

The following case study could be elaborated: (MATTHEW 18:1-11)

Subjects: Jesus, child, children, disciples, humankind, angels, Heavenly Father.
Objectives: To demonstrate the primary steps into the Kingdom of Heaven:
To show who is the greatest in the Kingdom of Heaven.
To prove whom it is who receiveth Jesus.
To announce an activity of the children's angels.
To declare the purpose of the coming of the Son of Man.
Methods: To stage a real-life dramatization for the anxious critics.
To lecture warnings to the world.
Procedures for man to follow:
POSITIVE: For man to be converted by becoming as a little child.
For man to humble himself as that little child.
For man to receive one such little child in Jesus' name.
NEGATIVE: Whoso shall offend or despise one of these little ones which believe in Jesus shall take the consequences.
Results:
POSITIVE: Man shall enter into the kingdom of heaven.
Man is greatest in the kingdom of heaven who is as that little child.

Whoso receiveth one such little child in Jesus' name has received Jesus.

NEGATIVE: Or man should have a millstone hanged about his neck and be drowned in the depth of the sea.

Or man shall be cast into everlasting hell fire.

Declarations: That in heaven the children's angels do always behold the face of Jesus' Heavenly Father.

That the Son of Man is come to save whoever is lost.

In my classroom a reevaluation of broadening philosophies and practicalities is continually being made. Legal accuracies of pedagogical accomplishments and endeavors are undergoing rigid appraisal for validity and continuance.

In this framework of constant inventory, the individual students and teacher are allowed flexibilities to experience accelerated growth patterns of personal interests and achievements. Each person is free to explore, within the limits only of God and man's laws, his or her expectations of truth in proven and accepted research.

Any subject in existence may be thoroughly examined by each student to the extent of his or her interest and ability to grasp these truths and theories involved. Guidance may be sought beyond our school staff; doctors, ministers, and other authorities may be consulted.

"Hear counsel, and receive instruction, that thou mayest be wise . . ." (PROVERBS 19:20.)

"Even a child is known by his doings, whether his work be pure, and whether it be right." (PROVERBS 20:11.)

"In multitude of counsellors there is safety." (PROVERBS 24:6.)

Early in the school year all of my students soon realize that their individual responsibility for their own learning is continually evaluated in an atmosphere of security, respect and love. (Repeating a truth penetrates our learning processes.) Progress records are filed in the students' folders. All of their written work for the school year is kept for personal encouragement.

Conferring with the individual student alone is important. Later a conference with the student, parent and teacher is scheduled. Since the work under discussion involves the student accomplishing this progress, I find it best for all concerned, that he or she be given the honest opportunity of being included in the conference to again take the responsibility for his or her own learning with the full support of parents and teachers.

Always on the first day of school my telephone number is written on the board with my name, for time has proven that availability to students and their parents is rewarding. A security in peacemaking is established and the privilege has not been abused. Condemning students for immaturities doesn't make for as much progress as does patient, long-suffering reasoning. They soon learn the importance of hearing directions in school. They know that only the explained lessons are given for enrichment study, and they also know that a tracer can record their phone call.

There are times of stress that merit calls to or from home. We welcome early solutions. The record shows that this support reinforces our understandings.

Several years ago, a sixth grader who was frustrated in her home situation by drinking parents, confided in me her great fear and distress. Her father was threatening her, for his own motives, with her personal safety. Because her mother had been interested enough to attend a P.T.A. meeting, I prayed that this problem could be settled within the home and with the least amount of damage to reputations.

With the daughter's permission, I phoned her mother for approval to consult the daughter's minister. He had the spiritual authority to offer guidance to help protect this family in God's cleansing power.

The church community knows now that this family is restored in God's love, but they need never know the direct manner in which a connection was made through instruments

Let Us Reason Together

of God's guidance, how a near-tragedy was prevented. "Come, let us reason together."

Teachers, students, why dare we have a "no-religious" attitude in the classroom—with not even one Bible found in the 200 section of the Dewey decimal classification! Has your school library a Bible—the world's all-time best seller, the best one-volume library in existence?

As a child "in the Lord," I studied the Scriptures mainly in the King James Version of the Bible. Even though I own several other translations, the Holy Spirit teaches in the King James version as well. The beautiful wording, phrasing seem to capture a reverent, holy, and worshipful atmosphere. The individuality of our Lord is all along the Way. Praise His Holy Name!

Once I had a tense experience with a new teacher who was fervently working toward a master's degree. Unfortunately she accepted the word of students without clearing with the teacher. One Learning Lab youngster had accused me of forcing him to be isolated away from the classmates, and placing him against an outside wall. The other Lab student reported that he wasn't getting instruction in math, since he had to be out of class for special remedial studies.

This inexperienced teacher contacted the parents, and had them come to school to confer with the principal, without consulting me—the homeroom teacher. To be sure, I was a bit stunned, yet knew that I could easily establish the facts. "Therefore if thou bring thy gift to the altar, and there rememberest that thy brother hath aught against thee; Leave there thy gift before the altar, and go thy way; first be reconciled to thy brother, and then come and offer thy gift." (MATTHEW 5:23,24.)

In health class, we had had a discussion on advice from a veterinarian to never place an animal cage flat against or next to an outside wall for the coldness would penetrate the area and break down the animal's resistance. This would also apply to the human being when sitting or sleeping.

I never isolate a student for such discipline. He may have a arrangement and research space. Until a conference can be scheduled, he may be placed on assignment somewhere else in the classroom or in the school plant.

arrangement and research space. Until a conference can be separate study area because of the need of special material scheduled, he may be placed on assignment somewhere else in the classroom or in the school plant.

The other evasive student had placed in his folder several math pages of accomplishments that bore out the fact that instructions were continuing. A child's imaginations and disappointments can cause misinterpretations.

"Moreover if thy brother shall trespass against thee, go and tell him his fault between thee and him alone: if he shall hear thee, thou hast gained thy brother. But if he will not hear thee, then take with thee one or two more, that in the mouth of two or three witnesses every word may be established." (MATTHEW 18:15,16.)

If all of us would settle our problems as directed by the Scriptures, solutions would be forthcoming in God's power.

Fortunately, I have two cousins who are Christian attorneys who would advise me should legal action be necessary for my protection. Here again I strive to heed the teachings of the Scriptures: "Dare any of you, having a matter against another, go to law before the unjust, and not before the saints? Do ye not know that the saints shall judge the world? and if the world shall be judged by you, are ye unworthy to judge the smallest matters? . . . How much more things that pertain to this life? . . . All things are lawful unto me, but all things are not expedient: all things are lawful for me, but I will not be brought under the power of any . . . And God hath both raised up the Lord, and will also raise up us by his own power." (I CORINTHIANS 6: 1-3,12,14.)

The time of swift testing did come in torrents. Following a regular Instructional Television Program, the usual discussion of relating the subject to our studies was continued. This particular topic involved a briefing of witchcraft, spiritualism, and exploring mental capacities.

Only during the preceding week I had heard on national television and received in a newsletter the following statement by Reverend Leroy Jenkins:

Let Us Reason Together

The Bible says to work while it is still day, meaning the Spiritual door will be closed. Billy Graham, a great man of God who has won millions to the Lord, has brought this out in his services many times. Let us remember to pray for him, and also for our president, President Jimmy Carter. God told me four years ago to tell him that he would be president of the United States. I did. He said that I was teasing him. And now he is.

The students were especially impressed that this prediction had come forth. I asked them to investigate everything that they hear, and to establish for themselves truth and theory that is positive or negative. In this situation positive is that which builds up trust and security. Negativeness brings fear and insecurity. They gave every reaction of having enjoyed our class discussion as they trust their teacher to grant their every constitutional right and responsibility.

Since I am among the hundreds of cousins who proudly claim a documented relationship to President Jimmy Carter—five generations ago we had mutual grandparents, James Kay and Grace Elgin Kay—I was keenly interested in this prophecy being given before it was fulfilled.

The next day, the principal, with another teacher, and one sixth grade student came to my room after school hours for a preplanned conference. The boy's mother had phoned that she would not have any teacher repeating Leroy Jenkins in her son's classroom.

Immediately I told them that I would contact my attorney (a Christian) to verify that I was within my legal rights to have lead this discussion.

To avoid the fire of pressure, the boy was transferred into another classroom session. Yet later he was expelled from school for disobeying school policies.

I am fortunate to be able to keep up with the successes of many of my former students throughout the years. They will learn that *"today is the tomorrow that was planned yesterday."*

THREE

BEING IN THE WAY

Spiritual blessings were obvious in my childhood. My God-fearing parents trained their five children in the loving disciplines of scriptural teachings, in family devotionals and "living" in action in a full church program. Childhood was genuinely a happy time in my memory, especially so because of the love of my parents, who gave us as many opportunities as they could make available, and because of the devotion of my dear sisters and brothers. Along with the varied sports and musical training, I was encouraged to earn the ranks in the Girls Auxiliary of the Women's Missionary Society, from Maiden steps to the completion of Queen Regent; thus I studied and memorized many Scriptures.

While yet in high school, I discovered my fondness for teaching juniors in Sunday school and Vacation Bible School. Then soon as a lifeguard and camp counselor at summer camp, my expanding experiences confirmed this. During the college years, two summers were spent as a staffer at Ridgecrest Baptist Assembly. Here I continued a growing commitment to answer a strong yearning for a full time career in missions. Most of us agree that everyone's life's story could fill a book.

When I was graduated from Meredith College, a North Carolina teaching certificate in the elementary grades was another valuable possession. The years have proven that my foreign mission field calling has included a public school classroom. A strong spiritual interpretation has been accented in my sixteen

Being In the Way

years of teaching experience. I have felt a definite confirmation of my remaining in the public schools rather than accepting placement in a private Christian school.

During the informative year of teaching in a Jewish community in Atlanta, Georgia, a keen consideration was given to constitutional rights. Twenty-five students out of thirty were Jewish. Most of these exceptional young teenagers continued afternoon classes at their synagogue.

There was one certain David K. who had been born in the lineage of King David. As the Jewish prophecy has it until this day, David K. could have been their promised Messiah. After his twelfth birthday, the Jewish students concluded that this David was not the Promised One, yet he may become the father of the expected, they believe.

Without forcing convictions, the special holiday celebrations were beautiful times to exchange heritage experiences in loving kindness. The five Gentiles will know in Heaven how effective was their Christian witness.

" . . . The Comforter, which is the Holy Ghost, whom the Father will send in my name, he shall teach you all things, and bring all things to your remembrance, whatsoever I have said unto you." (JOHN 14:26.)

Following this special year in Atlanta city schools, I chose to experiment with an unusual opportunity that became available. During that particular summer, I visited my sister Jean and her husband in Winston-Salem, North Carolina. Joe was receiving his chaplaincy placement with the Home Mission Board of the Southern Baptist Convention. He was grateful for the excellent counselling training given to all ministerial candidates. And he encouraged me to participate in some of the counselling program, especially for spiritual enrichment.

By my own choosing, I began counseling sessions with a chaplain in the Pastoral Counseling Center, and with one of the Christian psychiatrists. Soon I accepted a teaching position in Winston-Salem, Forsyth County, in order that these valuable sessions could continue. A deeper prayer life and a better understanding of the Christian calling resulted from these experiences.

A more definite pattern of the Holy Spirit's activity had become more obvious in my life. Our Lord Jesus is real!

At the end of that school year, my dad became seriously ill. Mother had obtained her broker's license from the South Carolina Board of Realtors. My parents needed help. I was privileged in those few years to gain valuable experience in the business world of real estate, and to witness the loving bravery of my dad as His Father God called him to his Heavenly home.

Dad had served in the Medical Corps during World War I where he saw into Heaven during the death struggle of many of his comrades. He lived and died as a saint of our Lord. Even his surgeon wrote a letter of tribute after dad's homegoing.

Life was such that I had to have a deeper, more complete awareness of my Lord Jesus Christ. With our family business being terminated, and the homeplace being sold, I needed guidance from Heaven.

Yes, I pleaded prostrate before my Heavenly Father. I had known personal grief and disappointment. The tribulations of the heavenbound journey were real. With excellent health and a good education, I had to be sure of God's directions.

One weekday morning around six A.M. I was aroused out of my sleep by the strong voice of my dad calling from downstairs, "Elizabeth." Immediately I lifted my head. I know my dad's voice. I also knew that he was in Heaven. . . . While pondering and becoming fully conscience, the voice called my name again —"Elizabeth." I sat up in bed waiting to answer.

On the third calling of my name, "Elizabeth" in the stronger voice of another, my eyes turned straight ahead into the eastern window. In my spiritual vision, I saw a visitor—a heavenly being who glowed in a profound stillness. His form was covered with a heavenly white robe. His arms, hands were outstretched. My breath was stayed in these moments of ecstasy. His unspoken words were " . . . Peace . . . my peace I give to you . . . not as the world giveth, give I to you . . . Let not your heart be troubled. . . ."

A great passageway light shone straight up and out into a north easterly direction. This was holy ground. . . .

Being In the Way

Oh, the thrill, the elation, the reality of those moments. This vividness is in my conscious memory. This visitor was my Lord—the same One who will meet us at our homegoing on that great day.

I worshipped and praised God for this dynamic encounter. I thanked Him for the new peace of heart, and peace of mind that remains until this day.

Soon I bounded down the steps to share this reality with my dear mother. She was yet in bed. So I prepared our breakfast anxiously. As soon as time would allow, I phoned the church office for an appointment with my pastor, Dr. D.M. Rivers, Pendleton Street Baptist Church, Greenville, S.C., now retired. Graciously he listened to my excitement in describing this reality.

The pastor shared other experiences that friends had related to him. My security in the future had been crystallized. This truth had been claimed: " . . . ye shall abide in my love; even as I have kept my Father's commandments, and abide in his love. These things have I spoken unto you, that my joy might remain in you, and that your joy might be full." (JOHN 15:10,11.)

Since that memorable morning, I have read of a similar encounter in one of Kathryn Kuhlman's books. It is normal for maturing "children of God" to have many experiences when their spirits are quickened in Holy Spirit Power. Praise His Name!

The next several months revealed another need. Several applications had been made to private Christian and secular schools from California to New York. With no family responsibilities, I was free to go where there was a leading of the Lord. However, this need concerned a favorite aunt of ours who had become seriously ill in Charlotte, North Carolina.

When visiting with them, I learned of an opportunity to teach with the Charlotte-Mecklenburg Schools. My mother and I moved here, much in prayer, seeking where we would live and grow in spiritual opportunities.

Soon we realized that anyone living in Charlotte is living "on-stage" for this great city is blessed with diverse activities.

And known to us, where God's spirit is, there is action. Satanic attacks naturally are being made. Having experienced that Christ has already won the battle, we continue to claim victories with Him in the joy and excitement of living.

After hearing and reading similar testimonies about hundreds who encounter God's goodness and mercy in the spiritual and physical realms, in the great ministries of ordained servants of God whose lives hold a strong influence in this mighty city, I will freely share my found "joy in the Lord" without fear of consequences. On-stage here in Charlotte have been and are hundreds of God's chosen instruments: unnumbered saints who love God's calling, who await His coming in this great day of the expected rapture.

Another sacred experience can be shared with those who love His appearing. When I was seated next to her, my dear mother was pointed out in the audience by Reverend Ernest Angley during October, 1975, as the gift of knowledge was present: "The lady in navy is receiving a healing for an abdominal infection. Come forward and receive your complete healing." Mother stood immediately for she was on prescription for this infection. She walked on to the stage in Ovens Auditorium. As Brother Angley placed his hand on her head, she was overpowered in God's Spirit and was healed. Her doctor confirmed this healing. No longer did she take medication. Within weeks after this miracle, she made a trip, in full strength, to the Holy Land in December, 1975, with my brother Robert, his wife June, and three of their teenagers. We praise our Lord for his "goodness and mercy endureth forever."

" . . . be ready always to give an answer to every man that asketh you a reason of the hope that is in you with meekness and fear." (I PETER 3:15.)

FOUR

IF YE LOVE ME

"Therefore whosoever heareth these sayings of mine, and doeth them, I will liken him unto a wise man . . ." (MATTHEW 7:24.)

"Buy the truth, and sell it not; also wisdom, and instruction, and understanding." (PROVERBS 23:23.)

This particular school year's homeroom section alone would have been the choice heterogeneous grouping for analysis in my college days' study of Tests and Measurements. The varied forms of testings and evaluations had indicated the wide range of developed skills and potential abilities present.

One other teacher and I had a flexible schedule that combined team teaching and divided instructional sections, within two different classrooms for sixty sixth graders. A folding wall offered a variety of arrangements in our comfortable setting. With the combination of all subject areas, there was an unlimited scope in curricula.

With a concluding statement in the beginning of an evaluation, this was one of my best years of classroom experience. Answers and actions were always forthcoming. Cooperation for individual student progress was emphasized throughout the administrative and supervisory staves. There was an obvious attitude of learning at all levels.

Our Fred, whose mother is a former P.T.A. president, proudly states that he is part Cherokee Indian. One of his compositions gave some interesting reflections:

> *Today is January 5th. This morning, I studied my guide sheet, then took out my notebook and went to work. Research study is part of the action that my class does during the day.*
>
> *We all have maturing principles. We have positive conversations and plans. Everyday we are careful to leave our room in a neat order.*

Special discussion sessions were usually planned into our daily schedule, or they were extemporaneous. It was here, in these gatherings where interrogations were previewed and reviewed, where ideas were brought into focus, and concrete plans for research were established by the participants and the leader-in-charge.

On the first day of school, our sessions began with "School on the Moon—A.D. 2000." Some of the other open-ended discussions have been: Future Spaceage, F.B.I. Agents, The National Election in 1996, What If Everyone Played Chess?

The theory and/or truth approach used a combination of open-ended and educational analytic discussions in Tommy's session for his own selection: previewing Hal Lindsey's book *The Late Great Planet Earth*. (Several had seen Kathryn Kuhlman interview Mr. Lindsey on her national television program.)

Many classmates had noticeable influence in class meetings with their invaluable contributions:

> Brian, whose father is a fireman and an instructor, had an active influence on his classmates' thinking.
>
> Barry, the son of a high school principal, steadily became more flexible in expressing his thoughts in written composition, as did all of the students. Some of our research for discussions was in written form.
>
> Karen impressed us with her bravery when her father's life was in question at the time of a leg amputation. She had helped him in adjusting to his prosthesis.
>
> Marvin's father and Beth's grandfather are well-known ministers in the community.

The meetings proved to enrich preparations for visits from our school nurse, dietitian, Red Cross director, and other community leaders.

After an instructor from the Health Department explained to our student body the hazards of smoking, a dynamic film was shown. The students were given a challenge, then a booklet to help dissuade parents from smoking. You can imagine the reaction that some parents gave amidst the pleas of some of the students.

We also had concentrated discussions in Basic First Aid classes. This inquisitive approach is a clincher for igniting thought and action. Most of these students received credit from the American National Red Cross.

During the first week of school, our Mark often was fast asleep by 9:30 A.M. if he had not had a fight and/or had come to class thirty minutes later. Conferences were soon arranged by the office to check the fightings and smokings in which he was involved.

When his parents came for consultation, we learned of Mark's inability to sleep easily before midnight. Also, that his handicaps seemed to be innumerable. Both of the parents were severe, and were habitual smokers. Mark had a record of being frequently paddled at home. He had an inferior background of knowledge in all subject areas. There had not been a visit to the family doctor for years "because he seemed to be well."

We had not spared the rod of loving, kind discipline, and spoiled Mark. His doctor treated him for a nervous condition. He went on to become an outstanding ball player. All of his subject areas showed steady progress as regular conferences, with commitments, continued with Mark, his parents, and teachers.

Early in the semester, circumstances forced us to study the lives and responsibilities of policemen-women and the Federal Bureau of Investigation. Some of our students had received threats from a few upperclassmen. When assured of confidential protection, and of a fast-growing knowledge of values in the safety of school and community, the students grew in cautious boldness.

Our guidance counselors will confirm how reliable many of our students became in sighting trouble spots quickly and quietly to help avoid further disturbances in the buses, restrooms, and elsewhere.

Our students, by the end of the first semester, were fast gaining experience in research that follows the scientific procedures of investigation from the known into the unknown, into established truth and theory. The frequent class meeting sessions of many descriptions were scientifically proven to be successful.

At the time of this observation, the several problem-solving sessions had concluded with the opinion that each individual accept the responsibility of his own growth in every phase of his entire program, with guidance when needed. We sought to unite in effort and in enthusiasm to succeed in all of our endeavors, especially when purposes are established and research is continued.

Progress became more specific when a chart was inked, listing the students' conclusions for successful research. Frequent referral to this list brought noticeable response. A protective atmosphere surrounded our activities. The individual student's needs were being met more thoroughly, and the entire outlook continually gained confidence, strength, and vision.

"Study to show thyself approved unto God, a workman that needeth not to be ashamed rightly dividing the word of truth." (II TIMOTHY 2:15.)

"He that hath my commandments, and keepeth them, he it is that loveth me: and he that loveth me shall be loved of my Father, and I will love him, and will manifest myself to him." (JOHN 14:21.)

FIVE

RENDER TO CAESAR

Jesus set this example by His words and action: "And when they were come to Capernaum, they that received tribute money came to Peter, and said, Doth not your master pay tribute? He saith, Yes. And when he was come into the house, Jesus prevented him, saying, What thinkest thou, Simon? of whom do the kings of the earth take custom or tribute? of their own children, or of strangers? Peter saith unto him, Of strangers, Jesus saith unto him, Then are the children free.

"Notwithstanding, lest we should offend them, go thou to the sea, and cast an hook, and take up the fish that first cometh up; and when thou hast opened his mouth, thou shalt find a piece of money: that take, and give unto them for me and thee." (MATTHEW 17:24-27.)

"Render therefore unto Caesar the things which are Caesar's; and unto God the things that are God's." (MATTHEW 22:21.)

In our citizenship sessions, our students become more fully aware that there are constitutional rights and responsibilities for all students, parents, and teachers. In beginning our school year we review the history of every subject to strengthen the foundation of our understandings.

The encyclopedia in our homeroom library includes in the listings of the heritage of Western civilization the influence of Christianity, right along with "Greek reason set men free"; Magna Carta (earlier laws among the Britain were found to be laws of Biblical concepts); English Bill of Rights; French Declaration of the Rights of Man; and on to our American

Declaration of Independence, and the United States Constitution, which has been considered as one of the most outstanding compositions ever composed by the minds of men.

What is being stressed here in this chapter is that students have a right to honestly investigate their legal heritage which does, by the facts of history, include a strong influence from Biblical truth.

I have observed firsthand, on the scene, that some of our so-called best schools have a no-religious attitude. They completely ignore any item that has a tone or suggestion of any religion. Their library shelves contain no religious books. A Bible is not to be found on the school property. The faculty is sterile in their pretenses as a false presentation is given to our youth.

Yes, a teacher, as an employee of the state government, does not advance the practice of any religion by forcing beliefs or by indoctrinating students. The teacher does not require school prayer or devotional Bible reading. The teacher does not advance or inhibit religion.

Teachers can present, however, a study of what the various religions believe—comparative religion, religion in history in relation to the advancement of civilization; the reading of the Bible for its great literary selections and historic qualities as part of secular training in the curriculum; the variety of philosophies expressed in literature, music and art which have as their subject the Deity, as the testimony expressed by the composer. All of this is maintained in order to accomplish a balanced and genuine educational program.

The First Amendment secures the right of an individual to practice his religion as long as he doesn't interfere with the school's schedule. His right to pray is also his legal right, and time (a moment) can be provided in his schedule for this. Because of being an American citizen, and because attendance at school is compulsory, a certain sacred legal right can be claimed by the student—the free expression of religion.

Throughout the school in which I presently teach, a practice has developed to enhance in-depth concentrated reading interests. For thirty minutes, once a week, our sixth graders each read silently, all at the same time, a positive reading selection made by personal choice. This period is their time for pleasure reading when no assignments are due. Occasionally I've seen some of them reading, by choice, from their own New Testaments.

Within our schedule there are times especially accented for aesthetic development. During this time our cultural subjects—music, art, and literature are enjoyed. Again here is an opportunity for developing student leadership—a choice to make for the pleasure of others:

> One student planned for us to "draw" what we heard in color while listening to the Grofé's *Grand Canyon Suite*. All of these drawings were mounted and arranged on one of the bulletin boards by the students.
>
> Another student illustrated Joyce Kilmer's poem "Trees" in art and music.
>
> Later a boy chose to read from the Gospel of St. Matthew before having us listen to his record, "The Lord's Prayer."
>
> During this patriotic year, another boy chose to quote from memory the Preamble to the Constitution.

These are examples of the variety of planning that naturally comes forth from talented youngsters.

Anything whatsoever that a student wants to study beyond our basic subject presentation, is provided. If we don't have the information available, we consult an authoritative source. Our school nurse presents a recommended session for sex education with the written consent of each student's parent or guardian.

Most of our students are happy, mainly because they are learning and their problems are being solved. If someone rebels, it is usually until stronger understandings are developed.

My definition of Caesar's camp would include all of those who reject the teaching of our Lord Jesus Christ—the full, complete gospel in the revelation of His Heavenly Kingdom: Jesus Christ, the same yesterday, today, and forever. (HEBREWS 13:8.)

The Caesar era seems to have gone into some of today's

churches, for some of the proclamations are blind to the manifestation of God's Holy Spirit in the very lives of God's anointed servants. With explained documented evidence by anointed physicians and scientists, that the fruits and gifts of the Spirit are in action as taught in the Scriptures, some of our educators will not examine the facts, the truth. They blindly deny the evidence and condemn these blessings.

A stern warning is given in God's judgment on these false teachers: "And David said . . . Destroy him not: for who can stretch forth his hand against the Lord's anointed, and be guiltless?" (I SAMUEL 26:9.)

In the dramatic twelfth chapter of Matthew, in rebuking these false religious teachers, Jesus' condemnation was severely clear: "O generations of vipers, how can ye, being evil, speak good things?" The great chapter ends with our Master's gentle invitation: "For whosoever shall do the will of my Father which is in heaven, the same is my brother, and sister, and mother." (MATTHEW 12:50.)

SIX

LORD, TEACH US TO PRAY

"And when thou prayest, thou shalt not be as the hypocrites are: for they love to pray standing in the synagogues and in the corners of the streets, that they may be seen of men. Verily I say unto you, They have their reward.

"But thou, when thou prayest, enter into thy closet, and when thou hast shut thy door, pray to thy Father which is in secret: and thy Father which seeth in secret shall reward thee openly . . . : for your Father knoweth what things ye have need of, before ye ask him.

"After this manner therefore pray ye: Our Father which art in heaven, Hallowed be thy name. . . ." (MATTHEW 6:5-13.)

Following the Supreme Court's decisions in Engel v. Vitale 370 U.S. 421 (1962), the office of the U.S. Attorney General made this statement, among others, to help clarify court actions: "These decisions do not in any way restrict the right of private individuals or groups to pray, but are aimed at the use of power of government to channel religious observances into prescribed official forms."

Prayer in the public school classroom has to be exceedingly controversial for several states to have allotted moments for silent meditation of the individual's choosing, as allowed by the U.S. Constitution and interpreted by the Supreme Court; and for other states to remain neutral, without including the topic of prayer in their state statutes books.

Whenever a legal action allows an opportunity for Spirit-baptized Christians to honor their Lord God, the fullest margin should be utilized.

After studying the courageous account of Rita Warren in *Mom, They Won't Let Us Pray*, A Chosen Book, I reviewed more fully why we have this privilege to meditate in public schools:

> Chapter 71, Section 1A, of the General Laws of the Commonwealth of Massachusetts has been amended to have at the commencement of the first class each day a period not to exceed one minute of silence for meditation or prayer.

The students in my home room class have appreciated having their moments of meditation, reverent silence, before we leave our classroom for lunch. (This time of day has legal clearance, as expressed by one of our Board Attorneys.) Those who are accustomed to praying a blessing before lunch may at this time exercise their freedom in a quiet setting. Some, by choice, bow their heads at the table before eating and pray silently.

This has a calming, organizing effect upon the entire class. Eyelids may be closed as they wish. Silence always is forthcoming out of respect for this privilege. Our digestive systems are more relaxed. We are more content, and thankful for our rights being protected. A time is provided (not required) for this religious freedom.

Anyone who opposes the "moment of meditation" will have to endure their objection, for the school is to be neutral in response to this legal privilege.

At no time have I sought to persuade a student to accept my convictions by imposing my prayers or Bible study meditations during classroom time in a public school. This would be training a child to break the law.

Personally, I would not want a teacher of another faith to pray with or interpret Scripture for my child. For a Jehovah's Witness to pray that the rapture had already occurred would be completely false, for this is scientifically impossible. The

Lord, Teach Us to Pray

entire Bible revelation would be out of joint. Prophecy is being fulfilled in God's time by His Word. The rapture, the coming of our Lord to catch us into heaven, has not, as yet, taken place. " . . . And he shall send his angels with a great sound of a trumpet, and they shall gather together his elect. . . ." (MATTHEW 24:29-31.)

"For verily I say unto you, Till heaven and earth pass, one jot or one tittle shall in no wise pass from the law, till all be fulfilled." (MATTHEW 5:18.)

Today's pace and problems are ofttimes thrust into the laps of our youth. Too often, they are given situations that many adults have never faced.

One dear girl transferred into our section with frustrations from a weak academic background, separation of parents, and the cancerous illness of her mother. It was obvious that she needed more security than could come from the helpful counseling sessions.

Our excellent counselor patiently encouraged her, yet she preferred to discuss her anxieties with a women and naturally talked with me. During one of her telephone calls, I was led to use this opportunity to ask for a greater strength. Since she and I were of the same religious denomination and she of a growing faith, I claimed my rights as a U.S. citizen, and as a child of God to pray with her on the phone away from school time and school property. We claimed our Lord's promises during this time of suffering. Our relationship was growing stronger when news came of her father's death.

During the remaining months, her academic average became the desired grade-level rating. Her mother came for conferences, and asked to join with us in praying for God's blessing of healing. She began watching Healing Services on television with plans to attend one of many of these priveleges (Miracle Services) here in Charlotte. She expects complete healing. . . .

One year later Teresa came to my classroom to report that her mother is well. Her doctor gave her a clean bill of health, and we are thankful.

Yes, a teacher's mission field is where she is, as she respects our great individual freedom as proclaimed in our profound Constitution, and as she respects Caesar's territory amidst our Lord's creation.

If anyone would contest this action of mercy, love and support, they would have to experience, more fully, the love of God.

"Likewise the Spirit also helpeth our infirmities: for we know not what we should pray for as we ought: but the Spirit itself maketh intercession for us with groanings which cannot be uttered. And he that searcheth the hearts knoweth what is the mind of the Spirit, because he maketh intercession for the saints according to the will of God.

"And we know that all things work together for good to them that love God, to them who are the called according to his purpose." (Romans 8:26-28.)

For those of you who think that you do not believe in praying in an unknown language, please explain the intercessory groanings of the Holy Spirit as the prayers of the saints are translated, prepared for our Lord God's presence in "golden vials full of odours." (Revelation 5:8.)

As I pray silently in the Spirit in my classroom, in an attitude of "praying without ceasing," God's comforting Counselor is there with me. Yes, I have been met with Satanic spirits that have possessed some of these young people, and victories have been claimed with this gift blessing of the Spirit.

Now some of you who are reading this cannot begin to understand what is being explained. " . . . the natural man receiveth not the things of the Spirit of God: for they are foolishness unto him: neither can he know them, because they are spiritually discerned. But he that is spiritual judgeth all things. . . . For who hath known the mind of the Lord, that he may instruct him?" (I Corinthians 2:14-16.)

If God's strength was not with me, I could not possibly teach twelve-year-olds. They are dynamos of precocious complexities.

For years I have exercised this blessing, this gift to pray silently in the presence of a disturbed, distraught student, as

Lord, Teach Us to Pray

we strive to reason together, in the name of Jesus, my Lord, for Satan to depart. As Jesus quoted Scriptures in the wilderness, I continue quoting.

For times beyond counting, I have known when many of my pupils have been delivered. I haven't broken a law of the country. Jesus came to fulfill the Law.

My Lord God hears my silent pleas. His promises are claimed even during the times when the tares are in the wheat, and it may be difficult to discern the spirits. My Lord delivers me from evil, and I sing praises to His Holy Name.

Our Jeff was really carried away with the casting out of demons that he had watched on national television. During breaktime he would jokingly "land" his hand on someone's forehead and command evil spirits to flee from him. Of course much laughter would follow.

I asked Jeff had he been scientific about his observation. In whose name-strength-power did these certain people claim to take authority to commit such an action? What had been the results? Had he, Jeff, considered all information available on the subject?

A sobering research resulted with knowing response.

SEVEN

ASK, SEEK, FIND

Because of the omnipotent, omnipresent, and omniscient nature of God, the entire system of education is impregnated with the total truth conception of our Master Creator. This conceivability cannot be aborted by the legal actions of any court in the land.

There are basic equations in the physical, mental, and spiritual realm that are eternally true: (Matthew 7:7,8.)

Ask=Receive
Seek=Find
Knock=Opened
Our Lord stands and knocks at your door.=If you will hear his voice and open the door=He will come in to you, and will sup with you=you will sup with Him. To him that overcometh=will sit with our Lord Jesus in His throne. Jesus overcame=is now set down with our Father on His throne. (REVELATION 3:20,21.)

There can be a miscarriage of truths by false teachers. " . . . slew in Judah an hundred and twenty thousand in one day, which were all valiant men; because they had forsaken the Lord God of their fathers." (II CHRONICLES 28:6.)

I respect, with a deep sense of obligation, the code of honor established by citizens in our free, pluralistic society. I am fully aware that the public schools are supported by nonbelievers and

Ask, Seek, Find 43

minorities as well as believers and majorities. Our study attitude in the classroom is free of pressure from any dictatorship. We are of a civic and patriotic stamina that strives to help the individual develop to his maximum capacities. I respect the intellect of each person to perceive, to choose among established truths, those qualities that will enhance his maturity.

Without pressure or force of harassment, his educational surroundings will contain unnumbered choices that he can make. If he chooses to serve the Lord God Almighty, Heaven in abundance is his forever. If he chooses to serve the prince of this world, damnation of his soul will result in this life as well.

The purpose of this writing is to accent, to proclaim afresh that the Christian worker is to be involved in politics, in public schools, in the world's activity, as a living witness to the Glory of God to whom these territories belong.

" . . . whatsoever is spoken . . . in the ear . . . shall be proclaimed upon the housetops." (LUKE 12:3.)

In a chapter of scientific research, evidence must be forthcoming. My teaching presentations have never brought a complaint from the parents of twenty-five Jewish students, from the parents of two Jehovah's Witness students, or from the acknowledged atheistic father of another student in previous years. Yet now, in recent times, freedom of speech and research is being forced into limits by nonChristian parents who have tried to restrict class discussion.

" . . . Woe to the inhabitors of the earth and of the sea! for the devil is come down unto you, having great wrath, because he knoweth that he hath but a short time." (REVELATION 12:12b.)

During these different school years, the plan of salvation has been presented in "growing" living by many students and teachers, as have many other modes of life (even self-worship). Our Lord God keeps the record. " . . . joy shall be in heaven over one sinner that repenteth. . . ." (LUKE 15:7.)

I can't keep a count of souls saved, for " . . . neither is he that planteth any thing, neither he that watereth, but God that giveth the increase." (I CORINTHIANS 3:7.)

Great minds in our civilization are given credit for stated truths which they claim to have originated. The valuable *Harvard Classics* and other works of renown, carefully attribute honor to the creative brain work of many outstanding great minds in history. The older I become, and the more knowledgeable, I pray, it does become clearer that our Creator God, in designing our marvelous bodies, planned for us, mankind, to have dominion over His creation on earth under His continual guidance. He knows the routes we must take, the plan we must follow to successfully reach our heavenly home in His protective power. God's clear and dynamic directions are to be fulfilled.

One year, my students and I, together, wrote our goals and objectives for the school year concerning math, science and health:

> To CONTINUE a preview/review approach to all phases of elementary grade math, science, and health concepts and values.
>
> To ESTABLISH a stronger background of experience in truth-theory progression from the known to the unknown.
>
> Thus, to apply the scientific method procedure in all study and research areas:
>
> To STATE the subject problem to be studied or solved.
>
> To GATHER all available materials and knowledge needed to prove the supposition.
>
> To EXPERIENCE the procedures necessary to complete a thorough investigation and examination.
>
> To DETERMINE the resulting conclusions according to truths and/or theory.
>
> To DELVE into the learning process beyond temporary memorization and/or mental impressions, to conquer permanent learning experiences whenever possible as a reservoir for future educational adventures.

During this important age, boys and girls need to better understand "from whence they came" (cause-effect relations) influences "withersoever thou goeth." The study of the theories

Ask, Seek, Find

and concepts of Creation, of evolution and of all of the great religious beliefs about life's origins, does not cause any problems. Students' interests are led to approach this as any other subject—to research, gather facts, opinions, consider all materials available including Harold Hill's book *From Goo To You By Way Of The Zoo*, and Dr. Robert E. Kofahl's *Handy Dandy Evolution Refuter*.

We believe that our Constitution gives us academic freedom in research study.

This report came in with a student early one morning. And later I checked for details with her parent: A Christian psychiatrist, while speaking at her church, had included a startling case report of a teenage patient who was at that time in a mental institution. This teenager has lost his mental soundness while indulging in Ouija board activity.

Other students contributed to the growing discussion by quoting the speaker's references to the scriptural judgment in Micah 5:12: "And I will cut off witchcrafts out of thine hand; and thou shalt have no more soothsayers." Time was given to a subject of their interest. They seemed satisfied with the discussion, and did not pursue the subject further.

Should a thorough research follow this inquiry, the laws of the state, opinions, and other results would be considered. Because of the growing accessibility of all types of books into the hands of teenagers, we strive to establish a cause-effect research into legal perspective.

Some few youngsters in our greater school area have had criminal records that have involved juvenile court action. Our students observe the results, and are informed that if they are found in possession of pot, and are convicted of possession, another word, felony, may be added to their vocabulary. Even if they receive a suspended sentence (all accounts, age, record, etc. included), they can be penalized for life by having lost a right to vote, to run for public office or to own a gun. They can lose their chance of ever becoming a lawyer, engineer, dentist, doctor, realtor or schoolteacher, etc. They can't have a job where they must be licensed or bonded. They are unable to work for the city, the county, or for the federal government. They cannot be enrolled at a military institution.

Stern warnings of these grievous consequences must be given along with the knowledge and trained skills of how to overcome temptations and forced pressures.

"And ye shall know the truth, and the truth shall make you free." (JOHN 8:32.)

If educators themselves would completely analyze the history of cause-effect of every influence, the truth of results would be obvious. For some five thousand years, where has Trancendental Meditation advanced the civilization in which it was originated? What gods does this program worship? What constitutional right have we to establish such a pagan religious practice in our public schools or elsewhere with taxpayers' money?

Minds of truth will come forth with positive answers and positive action.

Should you study a chronological time-line that has been prepared by our students and placed full length on a sidewall, you would at once sense from the beginning to A.D. 2000, a balance of posted eras, theories, facts, peoples, events, contributions, and predictions.

How, please, can any history class accomplish honest research unless a Bible, concordance, Bible dictionary, maps, et cetera are available along with some other several hundreds of books within the classroom or school libraries?

As we recognize contributions from the Far East, Middle East, Asia, Europe, and where ever else is needed, we find exciting contributions from the Bible that have had profound bearing on the history of where we are today. This cannot be denied.

Archaeological discoveries recently made in excavating Biblical cities reveal records found that confirm Biblical accounts as factual. Because of their natural interests and home training, many of these students can find the geographical area for the much talked about, prophesied Armageddon, the "Great Final Battle of the Ages." (REV. 16:16.)

Many of the following scientific truths, when contemplated, have stimulating enrichment:

Ask, Seek, Find 47

"Through faith we understand that the worlds were framed by the word of God, so that things which are seen were not made of things which do appear." (HEBREWS 11:3.)

"For the invisible things of him from the creation of the world are clearly seen, being understood by the things that are made, even his eternal power and Godhead . . . so that they are without excuse." (ROMANS 1:20.)

"Children in whom was no blemish, but well favoured, and skilful in all wisdom, and cunning in knowledge, and understanding science, and such as had ability in them to stand in the king's palace, and whom they might teach the learning and the tongue of the Chaldeans." (DANIEL 1:4.)

"I will . . . multiply my signs and my wonders . . ." (EXODUS 7:3.)

"Take this, and divide it among yourselves:" (LUKE 22:17.)

"He answered and said unto them, When it is evening, ye say, It will be fair weather: for the sky is red. And in the morning, It will be foul weather to-day: for the sky is red and lowering. O ye hypocrites, ye can discern the face of the sky; but can ye not discern the signs of the times?" (MATTHEW 16:2,3.)

These students draw the strong conclusion that scriptural and scientific facts are always in agreement.

During a challenging study of nutrition, our twenty-eight students helped prepare one selection from each of the basic food groups, with money from a school funded project: butter made in the classroom and served on crackers, popcorn popped in the room, "Sloppy Joes," and Waldorf salad.

Preceding this treat that was on the house, each student had prepared a day's menu with the calorie counts totaled and compared with each one's daily total need for strong healthy bodies, in consideration of proper exercise, rest, cleanliness and required medical care.

Our class submitted our "ten most wanted" menus to the dietitian, who graciously prepared those that could be adapted for the main school lunches. Other highlights of our Nutrition Unit included visits from a supervisory teacher, special orders of 16mm films, a planned tour of a meat packing plant, a lecture tour of the Hall of Health Museum, viewing the health series on Instructional Television, and a visit from our dental hygienist from the county Health Department. Handmade study booklets on the systems of the body included a chapter on nutrition. These were on display for one of our P.T.A. meetings. Interviews were made with the school nurse, the family physicians and dentists.

Some of our students already aspire to become professional nurses and dietitians.

One of their most revealing experiments was: A human tooth was dissolved in lemon juice in less than two months. This fact was forthcoming from their research: Eating too much pork can increase the aging process, for pork digests so quickly, it burns up energy faster than the body needs to tolerate.

All along the way, my students are asked to challenge everything that they read and hear. Proving the truth to themselves makes for independent thinking.

The program of health from the Scriptures concerns our *total health*—mind, soul and body:

"Beloved, I wish above all things that thou mayest prosper and be in health, even as thy soul prospereth." (III JOHN 2.)

"Wherefore I pray you to take some meat: for this is for your health. . . ." (ACTS 27:34.)

"Behold, I will bring . . . health and cure, . . . I will cure them and will reveal unto them the abundance of peace and truth." (JEREMIAH 33.6.)

The tender understanding of our Lord clears through in this beautiful consideration: "But Jesus said unto her, Let the children first be filled:" (MARK 7:27.)

"It is written, Man shall not live by bread alone, but by every word that proceedeth out of the mouth of God." (MATTHEW 4:4.)

"And we know that all things work together for good to them that love God, to them who are the called according to his purpose." (ROMANS 8:28.)

EIGHT

LEARN OF ME

" . . . I will give you rest. Take my yoke upon you, and learn of me; for I am meek and lowly in heart: and ye shall find rest unto your souls. For my yoke is easy, and my burden is light." (MATTHEW 11:28-30.)

Where there is truth in any realm, there is the character of our Lord. He made this claim: "I am . . . the Truth . . . ," the Person of Jesus Christ!

Teachers are fortunate to receive continual training and enrichment in all phases of their profession. Thus, we are privileged to draw from resources that have been inspired by truths from the ages, and to make stronger appeals that may capture our students' permanent responses.

The following description is a summary of another group's culminating accomplishments. These are similar to those of the previous year, yet uniquely different.

In our complete curricula, Section 6-0, of Art, Music, Physical Education, Mathematics, Science and Health, each student is encouraged:
1. To increase his ability to actively apply the methods of analytic thinking, and the actions of scientific researchers with emphasis on continual mental, physical, and spiritual exploration in a setting of establishing truths into the store of knowledge; however, he should realize that scientists agree that the ultimate truth has not been met in the scientific world.
2. To immediately seek identity, classification, and organization

within his entire environment of existing elements, powers, and destination—especially in the general realm of geometry, algebra, geology, chemistry, physics, biology, archaeology, etymology, ecology, astronomy, aeronautics and space exploration.

3. To continue developing student-leadership abilities and attitudes with a reverent, aesthetic respect for the state of existence, in an ever-present perspective, through assuming responsibilities in every available circumstance—striving to utilize the suggested experiences made by the authors of each textbook, the supplimentary teachers in art, music, physical education, educational television, and in any other media within the field of education.

4. To become more keenly aware of personal opportunities and responsibilities in a universal relationship, thus enriching our resources and enlightening our acumen through every known phase of communication and exploration: interviews, experiments, field trips, travels, hobbies, vocational facilities, and multi-media aids.

5. To concentrate, individually or in groups, attention on channels of growth and development by constantly exercising stronger study habits, learning skills, research techniques, and evaluations, with scientific thinking based upon logical and critical procedure, as a self-directed philosophy is being developed; and by employing, when desirable, the counsel of student-student/students, student-parent/guardian, student-teacher/teachers, counselors-principals/administrators.

My students usually began concentrated class discussions early in the school year to help strengthen their full school program. We met to plan, constructively criticize, and evaluate our entire program. These meetings were held regularly with the varied arrangements of chairs and desks or without furniture—standing or sitting on rugs, etc. Different students usually preplanned his responsibility in the discussion with a committee and/or teacher.

When we first became actively involved in the designed discussions, conversations were obviously intensified with the teacher leading in questions or statements that were to be elaborated. After hearing cassette tapings of these first discussions, an analysis was made of the subject and objectives accomplished —How? Why? Who? What? When? Where? The positive influence of the class discussion tapes, and the systematic planning together of the types and order of the meetings always helped to establish procedures rather smoothly. Additional mechanical orders were instigated. Students were trained to remain settled and not to move elsewhere after the discussions had begun. When they took turns speaking, it wasn't necessary to raise hands. Should they all speak at once, the leader raised a hand to remind them to cooperate by likewise raising hands and waiting to be called upon during any phase of the interrogation or elaborations.

Persistently our class discussions have focused attention on positive aspects with emphasis on results, destinations, and reactions. The simple, clear, analytic equations were restated. Every subject had an influence, in some way, on the entirety with procedure varying in hypothesis, research, experimentation, and diagnosis.

Topics of some of our discussions were in-depth previews/reviews of our year's study—You in the History of Earth, and Man in Relation to the Universe—theories/truths, positive/negative, past, present, and future perspective. Who are you?—genealogy; What are you?—biology, physiology; Why are you?—genetics; How are you?—psychology; Where are you?—geography, astronomy; When are you?—chronology. Additional suggested topics were: the progress of man, educational research, religions, politics, sports (land, air, water), intramurals, gymnasium, annuals, styles, safety, health, drugs, pollution, conservation, beautification, peace, legal rights and responsibilities of a twelve-year-old—eighteen-year-old, television, music, detectives, report cards, conferences, schedules, chewing gum, quiet, noise, school nurse, epilepsy, deafness, ear wax, eyes, glasses, cleanliness, teeth, calisthenics, signs, discipline, punishment, laws, without laws, careers, responsibilities, vacation, chess, checkers, hobbies, science fiction, time, synchronization, computers, the universe.

Some quotations for discussion have been: Art instructor,

"You're the loser, if you don't listen." School nurse, "Students should keep clean. Learn to bathe properly." Guidance counselor, "The student must learn ultimately how to teach himself. If he is educated, he either has knowledge or knows where to get it." American Red Cross Youth Director, "What do you know about the American Red Cross?" A science professor, "Scientists agree that the ultimate truth has not been met in the world of science," and he added, "or in the spiritual realm." Old Testament Proverb, "As a man thinketh, so is he." Also, "A wise man will hear, and will increase learning. . . ." Socrates, "Know thyself." Chinese proverb, "The deeper the river, the more silent the flow."

Book Reviews: *Reentry* by Dr. John Wesley White, Ph.D. Zondervan Books Edition, 1971, chapter 2, Science and Technology. Adventure story preview: *Little Pilgrim's Progress,* By Helen L. Taylor, Illustrated by W. Lindsay Cable. These books, among several hundreds of books from different libraries have been used for research study, pleasure reading and for oral discussion.

Other pertinent subjects have been: History: What After the Bicentennial? Etymology: Example—reaction by students to a comment made on educational television by an Indian who was being interviewed. He stated that the Islamic religion is a Christian religion. They challenged this statement—thus, there was further research on the origin of words.

One of our substitutes, an experienced teacher, agreed with us that our special sections have a high percentage of students with exceptional talents and resourcefulness. Reliable testings indicated ranges from the nonreader to those of tenth grade scoring, with one fourth of eighty-five students tested in an above average rating. However, the majority were hampered with a weak background of poor study habits and self-direction. A challenging task faced us during those formative months.

Even though frequently the same subject areas are or may be covered simultaneously in the different sectional groups, there is never any duplication of sectional procedures—naturally, because of individual differences.

Learn of Me

Observers noted that most of our students came to the discussion groups well prepared, and were enthusiastically expecting to think analytically and find results. Follow-through class sessions were in evidence for other discussions, interrogations, and conferences.

We are always rewarded when focusing our program on experiences which enlighten our perspectives and refine our accomplishments.

NINE

SPARE THE ROD

"Train up a child in the way he should go: and when he is old, he will not depart from it." (PROVERBS 22:6.)

The stage, the tempo is set for growth even during our first class session. With the background variety of all of the students, interest is soon aroused for investigations. Enthusiasm is ignited, hopefully, for grasping truths. Eagerness can be obtained for producing the desired results.

As previews of the school year are given, and reviews made of accomplishments, each individual is geared into action. With his or her academic background eventually strengthened and reinforced with workable knowledge, a happiness and satisfaction develop that have promoted a joy for learning. The students can be having so much fun at learning that understanding has overtaken them. Playing detective at learning is positive. Taking the responsibilities as an F.B.I. future agent helps to establish a code of honor. Claiming positive results instead of negative ones is the challenge.

Yes, there are times when real self-discipline is demanded to be happy in a math lesson at 1:30 P.M. when the natural man wants to nap after the inspirational session that follows lunch time.

However, when behavioral symptoms begin to appear, all of the students and the teacher, or the ones who have been involved, will soon have a discussion to reestablish the code of acceptable behavior. Reports may be given of the school policies on conduct. In citizenship classes, investigations can be made of the city-county-state laws and the origin of these, and the influence of these upon the formation of the laws of our country. This may include a review of governing laws from the Bible as well as from the entire history of man. A variety of enrichment opportunities are available: field trips to the city police department and jail; lectures from and conversations with patrol officers, et cetera. Always we reason together as a group or individually to weigh the problem against solutions and results.

Because of the tremendous positive results, I always find an appropriate time each year to help enlighten their understanding with another reality: Several psychologists have pointed out that children, young adults and adults of emotional immaturities may actually hit the one they admire or love, that sweethearts may fight each other in strong words, physical swattings and beatings. Grammar grade students, without fail, will heartily laugh at this observation as they recognize the unusual truth involved. Thus, "in-school" fighting rates become lower with understanding.

Seldom is a telephone conference necessary with the student/teacher/parent after the initial first conference. Yes, and by this, I mean going directly to the telephone any time of school day when the student cannot find a solution and continues to be disturbed. Talking directly with a parent over the telephone, with the student talking also, is most effective.

Should a parent admit that he cannot control his child at home, we urge the parents to join in conference in the Counseling Center. Some parents may need help personally as well.

Choices are always available as the count-down approaches. That is, by selfish choice or by causes of being disturbed, the student may refuse to cooperate, to be positive and progressive when understanding, counseling from the guidance counselor and/or Center is provided. In this framework of thorough reasoning, it is rare that a student will force a showdown of how his teacher really will respond. Soon all parents understand that foolishness for an "attention-getter" cannot be allowed. When any student, having been told well in advance, refuses to cooperate, he will take his desired consequences, for he knows in our classroom what they will be.

If any part of teaching students is unpleasant that of paddling a ten-, eleven-, twelve-year-old does seem unnecessary. For by that age of growth a keener sense of truth and error has surely developed and the conscience has not been marred beyond recovery. Even though the conscience is not fully developed at this age, the individual will test authority to learn his boundaries. If he refuses to use his reasoning ability, a stronger measure of outside of self-discipline is administered to help reach the inward self.

Personally, I am grateful to our Lord God for having guided us in procedures. When the rod of loving understanding in conference sessions is refused by the erring student, then the rod of pressure is not spared.

Again, how grateful I am that the courts of our land will allow the teacher, with the witness of another teacher, to explain first before the student again the reason for this punishment, in the hallway or elsewhere away from his or her classmates. The strokes are firmly given where no physical harm is done. The students receiving the corporal punishment are then required to sign an explanation of the incident.

As an active swimmer and tennis player, my right arm "gets the message across" usually in one application. Immediately the student develops a more solid respect for the loving authorities who strive to guide him into maturing self-reliance and self-respect that will help to promote society into a more positive production.

"Teachers may use reasonable force in exercising lawful authority." 115-146, *General Statutes of North Carolina 1971*.

Yes, thoroughness, patience, and persistent support must be constantly given by the teacher to afford every encouragement for this forthcoming adult behavior. When the pattern of acceptable behavior is established, I have only to look at a student for him to read my expression to understand that negative silliness will not be tolerated.

Some former students have thanked me for having required good behavior from them.

If any accounts being related in this writing seem to be

Spare the Rod

similar or in repetition, please know that this may be true. Also, please note the repetition in the Revelation: "To him that overcometh . . . will I give to eat of the tree of life . . . (Rev. 2:7.) To him that overcometh . . . will I give to eat of the hidden manna . . . (2:17.) He that overcometh shall not be hurt of the second death . . . (2:11.) And he that overcometh, and keepeth my works unto the end, to him will I give power. . . ." (2:26.)

Here is an account of another year's progress report. Discipline problems were more easily cleared with student-parent-teacher conferences during the first semester. It wasn't until February that assistance was requested from our guidance counselors. A peculiar rebellion developed which involved a shift of allegiance. Normally our dependable students would report any disturbances to a teacher. A deep silence, which pervaded the scene for a week, was interspersed with frequent disorders which we had not had previously—fighting, cursing, opening each other's lockers, stealing, misplacing books. Hall patrols were placed to help calm some of the pressures. Behavioral-problem discussions continued with those who wished to join the oral discussions. Those who refused to participate remained at their desks in independent study for a few days. Then all of them had written "discussions" which helped to clear the problems. Some of them would write on paper what they would not say aloud. We had successfully discussed disciplinary procedures whenever necessary. At this time, however, because of false accusations, temper flares, and threats, some of the parents had given their sons permission to fight, while disregarding the Code of Discipline of the School District—a copy of which each student had taken home earlier. Parents can undermine progress unintentionally. Parents were contacted and cooperation continued. Most of our students are now convinced that problems could easily have been solved had they calmly settled disagreements or properly reported them.

A new transfer from another school district came to us late in the school year with many negative patterns. Fortunately, the class was well trained by then, which gave me more time to escort him around as well as to find extra time for the required individual tutoring. Yet something was amiss. The expressions on the boys' faces were unusual, and no one would talk, especially when coming out of the rest room.

In emergencies, a teacher may go into a rest room unannounced. The small hallway from the larger hall gives the needed privacy. Once when the door was ajar, it was evident that disorder was present. With a firm reprimand, I soon thought that I had an understanding with the new fellow that our school policy allows no fighting, and has a hands-to-yourself stance. The temper of a twelve-year-old is no match for permanent injuries.

This case was immediately referred to the Guidance Center, where action was forthcoming. All rest room doors were removed from the hinges, and order began to return at once.

My reference for this prompt action was not only a knowledge of the city and state law, but a keen acknowledgement of the accurate teachings of Romans 1:21-28 " . . . when they knew God, they glorified him not as God, neither were thankful; but became vain in their imaginations, and their foolish heart was darkened. Professing themselves to be wise, they became fools, And changed the glory of the uncorruptible God into an image made like to corruptible man. . . .

"Wherefore God also gave them up to uncleanness through the lusts of their own hearts, to dishonour their own bodies between themselves: Who changed the truth of God into a lie, and worshipped and served the creature more than the Creator, who is blessed for ever. Amen.

"For this cause God gave them up unto vile affections; for even their women did change the natural use into that which is against nature; And likewise also the men, leaving the natural use of the woman, burned in their lust one toward another; men with men working that which is unseemly, and receiving in themselves that recompence of their error which was meet. . . . God gave them over to a reprobate mind. . . ."

TEN

BE YE PERFECT

"Which is Christ in you, the hope of glory: Whom we preach, warning every man, and teaching every man in all wisdom; that we may present every man perfect in Christ Jesus:

"Whereunto I also labour, striving according to his working, which worketh in me mightily." (COLOSSIANS 1:28,29.)

"But when that which is perfect is come, then that which is in part shall be done away." (I CORINTHIANS 13:10.) "For this corruptible must put on incorruption, and this mortal must put on immortality . . . then shall be brought to pass the saying that is written, Death is swallowed up in victory." (I CORINTHIANS 15:53,54.)

There would be disillusionment in thinking that we can live in a state of perfection in this life, for we cannot. Perfection is present only in the power of the Holy Spirit.

The Bible gives detailed instructions on maturing from babyhood into the waning years of this earthly life into Heaven; then strongly declares involvement and great activity in the life beyond death.

" . . . Of whom we have many things to say, and hard to be uttered, seeing ye are dull of hearing. For when for the time ye ought to be teachers, ye have need that one teach you again which be the first principles of the oracles of God; and are become such as have need of milk, and not of strong meat. For every one that useth milk is unskillful in the word of righteousness: for he is a babe.

But strong meat belongeth to them that are of full age, even those who by reason of use have their senses exercised to discern both good and evil." (HEBREWS 5:11-14.)

Self must be constantly dealt with, refreshed, replenished in the praises to our Lord, in His anointing power.

"Either how canst thou say to thy brother, Brother, let me pull out the mote that is in thine eye, when thou thyself beholdest not the beam that is in thine own eye? Thou hypocrite, cast out first the beam out of thine own eye, and then shalt thou see clearly to pull out the mote that is in thy brother's eye. For a good tree bringeth not forth corrupt fruit; neither doth a corrupt tree bring forth good fruit. . . . A good man out of the good treasure of his heart bringeth forth that which is good; and an evil man out of the evil treasure of his heart bringeth forth that which is evil: for of the abundance of the heart his mouth speaketh." (LUKE 6:42-45.)

"Create in me a clean heart, O God; and renew a right spirit within me." (PSALMS 51:10.)

If you lack God's favor and His intervention in your classroom, you need to follow His plan for you—for all of us:

"Behold, the Lord's hand is not shortened, that it cannot save; neither his ear heavy, that it cannot hear: But your iniquities have separated between you and your God, and your sins have hid his face from you, that he will not hear." (ISAIAH 59:1,2.)

"Now concerning spiritual gifts, brethren, I WOULD NOT HAVE YOU IGNORANT. . . . Now there are diversities of gifts, but the same Spirit. And there are differences of administrations, but the same Lord. And there are diversities of operations, but it is the same God which worketh all in all. But the manifestation of the Spirit is given to every man to profit withal.

"For to one is given by the Spirit the word of wisdom; to another the word of knowledge by the same Spirit; To another faith by the same Spirit; to another the gifts of healing by the same Spirit;

"To another the working of miracles; to another prophecy;

Be Ye Perfect

to another discerning of spirits; to another divers kinds of tongues; to another the interpretation of tongues:

"But all these worketh that one and the selfsame Spirit, dividing to every man severally as he will. For as the body is one, and hath many members, and all the members of that one body, being many, are one body: so also is Christ. For by one Spirit are we all baptized into one body, whether we be Jews or Gentiles . . . and have been all made to drink into one Spirit. For the body is not one member, but many. But now hath God set the members every one of them in the body, as it hath pleased him.

"Now ye are the body of Christ, and members in particular. And God hath set some in the church, first apostles, secondarily prophets, thirdly teachers, after that miracles, then gifts of healings, helps, governments, diversities of tongues. . . . But covet earnestly the best gifts and yet shew I unto you a more excellent way.

" . . . Rejoiceth not in iniquity, but rejoiceth in the truth; Beareth all things, believeth all things, hopeth all things, endureth all things. . . . For we know in part, and we prophesy in part. But when that which is perfect is come, then that which is part shall be done away. . . . And now abideth faith, hope, charity (love), these three; but the greatest of these is charity (love).

" . . . Even so ye, forasmuch as ye are zealous of spiritual gifts, seek that ye may excel to the edifying of the church. For God is not the author of confusion, but of peace, as in all churches of the saints. . . . Let all things be done decently and in order." (I CORINTHIANS 12,13, and 14; ROMANS 12:1-21; EPHESIANS 4:1-32.)

In attending Miracle Services for several years, I continue to marvel at the individuality of God as His splendid nature and character are being revealed. My first large service was in the huge audience with Kathryn Kuhlman in Atlanta, and later in Greensboro, N.C. Our Lord uses anointed servants who are submitted to His control as all of the gifts of the Spirit are manifested. The heaven of it all almost transforms you into the Celestial City. In the tremendous array of God's glorious power, you make your claim: "He who hungers and thirsts after righteousness shall be filled."

After intense observation, participating, and experiencing gifts (blessings) in the Spirit, I can rejoice and proclaim that our Father's promises are being fulfilled. I live, moment-by-moment in the renewing joy of experiencing afresh the "quickening in the Holy Spirit" as our Lord reveals His power to His Glory.

" . . . these signs shall follow them that believe; In my name. . . ." (MARK 16: 17-20.)

"It is a fearful thing to fall into the hands of the living God." (HEBREWS 10:31.)

"Aside from supernatural manifestations, such as angelic announcements, virgin birth, the star that guided the wise-men, Jesus passing through hostile mobs, cleansing the temple, his transfiguration, soldiers falling, darkness at the crucifixion, the veil rent, the tombs opened, the earthquake, Jesus' resurrection, angel appearances, there are recorded thirty-five miracles which Jesus wrought: 17 Bodily Cures, 9 Miracles over Forces of Nature, 6 Cures of Demoniacs, 3 Raised from the Dead, and other innumerable miracles indicated. . . .

"The method of the miracles were usually wrought by the act of Jesus' will, or by his word; sometimes by his touch, or the laying on of his hands. Occasionally he used saliva.

"The purpose of the miracles implies an exercise of creative power. They were a part of God's way of authenticating Jesus' mission. Jesus said that if he had not done works that no other ever did, they would not have had sin (JOHN 15:24), thus indicating that he regarded his miracles as proofs that he was from God. Then, too, his miracles were the natural expression of his sympathy for suffering humanity."*

---

*Copyright © 1965 by Halley's Bible Handbook, Inc. Reprinted by permission.

ELEVEN

YE SHALL RECEIVE POWER

"Have ye received the Holy Ghost since ye believed?" (ACTS 19:2.)

"But ye shall receive power, after that the Holy Ghost is come upon you: and ye shall be witnesses unto me . . . unto the uttermost part of the earth." (ACTS 1:8.)

There is no other writing, or source in existence that promotes the value of the individual "from here to eternity" as totally as does the Scripture, and to the very soul of the subject. Jesus Christ gave His entirety, the greatest love, to "whosoever believeth in him should not perish, but have everlasting life." (JOHN 3:16.)

The individual character traits and virtues that are emphasized in the health textbook . . . all stem from Biblical teachings:

"But the fruit of the Spirit is love, joy, peace, long-suffering, gentleness, goodness, faith, meekness, temperance: against such there is no law." (GALATIANS 5:22.)

" . . . whatsoever things are true, whatsoever things are honest, whatsoever things are just, whatsoever things are pure, whatsoever things are lovely, whatsoever things are of good report; if there be any virtue, and if there be any praise, think on these things.

"Those things, which ye have both *learned*, and *received*, and *heard*, and *seen* in me, *do*: and the God of peace shall be with you." (PHILIPPIANS 4:8,9.)

Many educators have copied from the Scriptures God's basic values and concepts, and have failed to give Him the credit by not listing the Bible in their bibliographies.

As explained in an earlier chapter, the scientific method of research came from His Word. Also therein is described: individual instructions, academic inquiries, the learning process, study procedures, problem-solving skills, decision making, motivating abilities, coordinations, analytic thinking, testing preparation, character training, intergroup education, socializing, communication, joyfulness in maturing experiences, and the basic concepts in educational psychology.

I am satisfied that the rudiments of learning mentioned here can be exemplified with Scriptures. However, the entire Bible must be studied continually as the Holy Spirit teaches us the fulfillments of the Word in personal experiences. One does not divorce all existing truth, knowledge in the world from the truth, knowledge spoken of in the Bible, for where there is truth . . . there is the Triune God as part of His totality. He proclaims this in the written word.

As we often read, our base of knowledge is continually increasing. This chapter alone is the subject for a complete book.

In one concise, conclusive sentence, our Master teacher gave us "the Golden Rule:" "Therefore all things whatsoever ye would that men should do to you, do ye even so to them: for this is the law and the prophets." (MATTHEW 7:12.)

Jesus developed his subject from an introduction to its conclusion with emphasis on essentials and involvements. He ultimately sought complete participation from each hearer:

"Go and do likewise." (LUKE 10:37.)
"Ye will know them by their fruits." (MATTHEW 7:16.)

Especially in the Psalms and Proverbs—"short, popular sayings expressing a well-known truth or fact," . . . lo, the entire Bible, a variety of modes of individualized instructions are employed. Learning tasks, materials, and settings are established where studies are conducted. Instructional methods with rates of advancement are coordinated with learning experiences. The individuals are prepared psychologically. That is, when possible, they are freed from emotional blockage, depressions, guilts or any other negative factors that would hamper the flow of learning. Their storehouse of knowledge is constantly supplemented. A repertoire of skills and accomplishments are exercised. Continually, they are relating to their environment—local to universal.

THE PROVERBS: (Chapter One)

Subject: The proverbs of Solomon, the son of David, king of Israel.

Object: To KNOW wisdom and instruction; to perceive the words of understanding;

To RECEIVE the instruction of wisdom, justice, and judgment, and equity;

To GIVE subtilty to the simple, to the young man knowledge and discretion.

Why? A wise man will hear, and will increase learning; and a man of understanding shall attain unto wise counsels: To understand a proverb, and the interpretation; the words of the wise, and their dark sayings.

What? The fear of the Lord is the beginning of knowledge: but fools despise wisdom and instruction.

How? My son, hear the instruction of thy father, and forsake not the law of thy mother: For they shall be an ornament of grace unto thy head, and chains about thy neck.

When? My son, if sinners entice thee, consent thou not.

Where? My son, walk not thou in the way with them; refrain thy foot from their path:

Who? But whoso hearkeneth unto me shall dwell safely, and shall be quiet from fear of evil.

Individual concentration, permanent learning, correction, longevity, and an abundance of resources and blessings are exemplified in Proverbs 3:1-13.

Conditions and Results:

> My son, forget not my law; but let thine heart keep my commandments; For length of days, and long life, and peace, shall they add to thee.
> Let not mercy and truth forsake thee: bind them about thy neck; write them upon the table of thine heart: So shalt thou find favour and good understanding in the sight of God and man.
> My son, despise not the chastening of the LORD; neither be weary of his correction:
> For whom the LORD loveth he correcteth; even as a father the son in whom he delighteth.
> Happy is the man that findeth wisdom, and the man that getteth understanding.

Illustrations here capture the imagination, appeal to the senses, hold one's interest, and are more easily remembered.

Should anyone wish to have additional concrete examples of educational principles and procedures that are taught in the Bible, please write to us, or visit our classroom.

A cycle of the learning process could be: A student may read what he has written in a dictating unit, then listen critically as he prepares a revision. In this way, everything an individual writes at this time goes through the cycle of composition, speaking, listening, analyzing, editing, and rereading before the assignment is given to a teacher for suggestions, and then returned to the student for completion, and filing in our records for references. Everything the students accomplish within the nine month session is available for referral to enhance our acumen of knowledge, and to continually revise our charted program.

Please note the accurate development of this competitive skill. The narrative becomes a sermon. " . . . and rejoiceth as a strong man to run a race." (PSALMS 19:5.) "Know ye not that they which run in a race run all, but one receiveth the prize? So run, that ye may obtain. And every man that striveth for the mastery is temperate in all things. . . . I therefore so run, not as uncertainly; so fight I, not as one that beateth the air: But I keep under my body, and bring it into subjection. . . ." (I CORINTHIANS 9:24-27.)

The questioning techniques of Jesus and his followers provoked his hearers into the directions of ultimate growth or failure. Concentrated questioning procedures are highly successful in the classroom, especially as stimulants within the learning process. The prolonged mental stimulations of subjects presented in question form have frequently brought enthusiastic individual-group response into research that has produced obvious results, and perhaps, permanent learning. The individual's ego, whether humble, sincere, or full of the varieties of pride, responds with the attitude of knowing that his opinions are of value.

In an analysis of the success of this procedure, a background of experience is involved. Affirmative commitments that stimulate positive actions of all participants are secured. An evaluation on the feed-back of discussions shows that the students are attaining a more independent level of study.

My students, this year, are fortunate to have in the homeroom setting a dictionary for each student, a class library with some seven hundred books arranged in the Dewey Decimal System, including four different sets of encyclopedias. And in addition to this there are our well-stocked school and county libraries.

Early in the school year, an atmosphere is established of seek/find through the numerous interchanges for personal/group analysis to conferences/interviews. As explained in the curricula development, we reason together from the known to the unknown, from truths into theories, always searching for truths upon which to construct our work and play load, and our own responsibility for our own individual and group learning.

We are always striving to master basic skills. Reading and the other language arts fundamentals, and mathematical constructions are daily scheduled. Most of the students will complete all of the basic textbooks within the nine months' program. These bright minds are fed on into the next level as determined by their initiative and ingenuity. Forced learning without purpose can cause frustrations. Too much individual aloneness can cause isolation and maladjustments. Also, our teenagers need not be overburdened with the cares of this world. Yes, concerned, but not overanxious.

A wide variety of methods for presentations are used with a balance of student, teacher, and commercial displays in evidence.

Another debatable setting of concentration for indepth study is influenced by this stated truth:

" . . . We beseech you, brethren, that ye increase more and more . . . that ye study to be quiet, to do your own business, and to work with your own hands . . . ; that ye may walk honestly . . . and have lack of nothing. . . . Wherefore comfort one another with these words." (I THESSALONIANS 4:10-18.)

This fun experiment involves laughter as well as serious pondering. Select two students to play chess or checkers, and at the same time have one continually ask the other friend questions about his reading habits . . . such as, What type of selections does he enjoy most of all? When does he want to read? How often does he go to the library? etc. An answer must be given when a question is asked. The one who is answering these questions about reading is also asking questions about sports,—any phase of sports, just as long as he keeps asking questions and getting answers from his play partner.

At the same time, outsiders will be asking questions of these two players, about plans for out-of-school activities, holiday and summer vacation plans. All of this activity, questioning, and answering must continue steadily as the teacher could give the two students assignments that they are to write on the paper beside the chess-checkerboard.

At this point, if the experiment is successful, each of the two students can be said to have a "six-track" mind, not a "one-track" mind, for each is: (1.) playing a game (2.) asking questions of the other student (3.) answering questions from the other student (4.) answering questions from classmates (5.) reading assignments given from a teacher (6.) copying assignments from the teacher.

Our students enlarge their thinking capacities also with this fun approach. They play large-board chess on bath tile squares that were given to us by a tile company. They also play human chess by standing on rug squares given by a furniture company. Each player holds onto his identification card while two mastermind opponents call out the plays.

One of our school dads and his son built for us a sturdy stage floor, 8' by 5', within a strong frame 6' tall. Removable curtains and backdrops convert this cultural center into a variety of learning stations. With a carpet on the stage floor, we play games, read, study, plan, write drama, et cetera—in addition to living all over the room. And that includes hanging items from the ceiling, and possibily covering some of our windows.

Other maturing experiences have included: A student-teaching program in which our students visit other classrooms of lower grade levels, to help younger pupils grow in academic skills. We also have had high school students and teachers to visit with us for classes in French and Spanish. Occasionally we pause to gain perspective of our relationship to the NOW. At this time each student may write his or her autobiography in three time perspectives—the past, present, and future plans. A refreshing evaluation during a heavy work load will help to dissolve confusion. A day's visit to their next year's grade level is always a plus for maturity. Spending the main part of one day with seventh grade students gives our sixth graders immediate access into their future. They are alerted into a pride of belonging to the purpose of education.

The teacher is continually learning from the students as well as from the entire program. Ofttimes our current event publications will present new inventions, experiments, etc., that have not yet been published in a daily newspaper.

These talented youngsters know that you love them. They discern your honesty, manner, habits and speech/thought patterns. The influence of a teacher over her pupils can frighten one into cautious detailed planning where proof and purpose for decisions and actions can legally be established. This is no light responsibility. The happiness in loving all of the children, the gratifications of observing their contented growth, the reward of knowing that maturation is proven are blessings to enjoy forever.

As teachers follow many, many students on into adulthood, and see how prosperous many of them become—the joys of the teaching profession are genuinely real.

Our class members expect visitors in our school and classrooms. Among these are our superintendent, members of the Board of Education, parents and their friends, television cameramen, and other workmen. Our doors and windows are open, and we are going forward in assurance.

You cannot fail as you claim truths in the physical and spiritual realms. The Power who created the universe is helping to supply our needs.

In analyzing hundreds of quotations, the following have been considered. George Washington: "It is impossible to rightly govern the world without God and the Bible." Abraham Lincoln: "I believe the Bible is the best gift God has ever given to man. All the good from the Saviour of the world is communicated to us through this book." Daniel Webster: "If there is anything in my thoughts or style to commend, the credit is due to my parents for instilling in me an early love of the Scriptures. If we abide by the principles taught in the Bible, our country will go on prospering and to prosper; but if we and our posterity neglect its instructions and authority, no man can tell how sudden a catastrophe may overwhelm us and bury all our glory in profound obscurity." Patrick Henry: "The Bible is worth all other books which have ever been printed." Charles Dickens: "The New Testament is the very best book that ever was or ever will be known in the world."

From twenty-eight quotations from great works of literature, selections were made to be illustrated artistically. These two choices were formed with colorful Christmas wrapping foil:

"A word fitly spoken is like apples of gold in pictures of silver." (PROVERBS 25:11.)

"The fruit of the Spirit . . . ," (GALATIANS 5:22), a cluster of nine grapes, each labeled.

Twenty-eight planned subjects of their own choosing for soap-carving gifts to the parents; some selected crosses, doves of peace, and the fish symbol.

"For as he thinketh in his heart, so is he . . ." (PROVERBS 23:7.)

In another reference book in our class library, our students may read and study pictures of archaeological discoveries such as the uncovering of a school room in Ur, where Abraham lived. Found there were some one hundred fifty school exercise tablets with mathematical, medical, historical texts and one large tablet of a Sumerian verb and its Semitic equivalent.

Here's a question for you, the reader. In studying the origin of words, etymology, this point of interest is met. In general reading, conversation, or listening or even television, your attention is blasted with expressions such as, "Gee," "Jeez," "Gosh," et cetera, all of which I have heard, stem from the word Jesus Christ. In Matthew 5:37: "I say unto you, Swear not at all; . . . But let your communication be Yea, yea; Nay, nay: for whatsoever is more than these cometh of evil." What then should be our response?

I could not be so deceitful as to ignore a great truth before my students that they may learn from one of the encyclopedias in our classroom: "A reference book which cannot be overlooked is the 'book of books'—the Holy Bible. It is not only the book referred to most often, but is the source of numerous other reference books that refer to it. The Bible is so important it is not surprising that there are in existence examples of every variety of reference book based on its subject matter. The complete Bible library includes the various authorized versions of the Bible as well as encyclopedias, dictionaries, atlases, handbooks, directories, indexes, concordances, and bibliographies concerned only with Bible lore."*

The Old Testament prophet Daniel in Chapter 12:4 foretold: " . . . even to the time of the end; many shall run to and fro, and knowledge shall be increased."

Scientists were stating in the early 70s that the world's knowledge is doubled every ten years, and printed materials every fifteen years. At present, the pace of increase is even greater.

Currently these itemized statistics were published nationally: Public school property losses in 1974 were over a half billion dollars: . . . vandalism, burglary, arson, student extortion, locker theft, et cetera.

Would that this ultimatum could be proclaimed from the housetop of Congress as it was during Solomon's reign from the Temple of God: "If my people, which are called by my name, shall humble themselves, and pray, and seek my face, and turn from their wicked ways; then will I hear from heaven, and will forgive their sin, and will heal their land." (II CHRONICLES 7:14.)

---

*Compton's Pictured Encyclopedia, 1966 ed., vol. 12, p. 131. Chicago: Encyclopaedia Britannica. Reprinted by permission.

TWELVE
GO YE...

"And they went forth, and preached every where, the Lord working with them, and confirming the word with signs following." (MARK 16:20.)

The following analysis of the recorded miracles of Jesus in the New Testament may be compared to His miracles of today as experienced and witnessed through His anointed servants and followers:

"The importance of Jesus' miracles lies not so much in the miraculous power which he displayed in them, as in the significance attached to them.

"In general they were effected by his simple word (MARK 1:27; 2:11) or touch (MARK 5:41) rather than by the use of magical devices.

"They did not bring glory to him, but were meant to bring glory to God (LUKE 7:16).

"They testified to God's love for suffering humanity (MARK 1:41;8:2).

"They fulfilled the Old Testament promises of the coming time of salvation when God would heal men's bodies as well as their souls (LUKE 7:22; ISAIAH 29:18-19; 35:5-6; 61:1).

"They were done in order to lead men to faith in the saving power of God at work in Jesus (MARK 9:23f.). They were not compelling signs of God's power: the Pharisees felt able to attribute them to the power of Satan (MARK 3:22). But to those with the eyes to see, they constituted the sign that God was at work in Jesus in fulfilment of his promises, and were meant to awaken and confirm faith in him.

"All this applies to the miracles of Jesus himself. It also applies to the miracles in the early church. The early Christians displayed powers similar to those of Jesus. We hear of sick people being cured, the dead being raised, the miraculous release of prisoners and even the power to inflict physical judgment. These were signs that the same power of God which was at work in Jesus was still at work in his disciples, confirming their message of salvation, and also warning of the reality of God's judgment."*

When a school teacher witnesses personal, inexplicable healings in her own family, she is enhanced with anticipation for additional miracles.

My sister-in-law, June Galphin Machen, has this beautiful testimony of God's Power in her life: "I give credit for my God-given healing to the prayers of dear friends, and to my loving family. But I felt the instant answer to the prayers of one especially anointed friend.

"Let's go to the beginning. My illness began over six years ago during the time I was looking after my mother who was dying with cancer in the hospital. This pain started just under my ribs on my left side during mother's illness. I kept trying to put it out of my mind for there was too much else to do to get sick with a family—my husband and four active teenagers. This continued on until after mother's passing, when it became unbearable. Twice I was rushed into the hospital, when the pain became so severe I could hardly breathe.

"After running many tests and X rays, they decided it was possible pancreatitis. I was put on a strict low-fat diet. At that time there really wasn't much else they could do when anything was wrong with your pancreas.

---

*Eerdmans' Handbook to the Bible, p. 520. Howard Marshall, The Guideposts Edition, 1973, W.B. Eerdman's Publishing Company. Reprinted by permission.

"Several more months passed and I was not any better. I was able to get into Emory University Hospital, Atlanta, Georgia, for more testings. After several days, my doctor called me into his office to go over the reports. He was so sorry to say it looked as though I had calcification of the pancreas and that there was really nothing they could do for this condition. He did have one more test to run, and wanted me to return the next day for the final report.

"That Wednesday night after prayer meeting, I saw this fine Christian friend who must have been led to walk on to our front door with us. I asked him to please pray for me, that I had something physically wrong that was very serious, and that I was to return the next day to Emory for the final report and decision on what to do next, if anything. He told me that he had some special Scripture he wanted me to claim, and that he would be praying for my healing. He went home and called me back to give the Scripture, I Peter 3:12. I had the most relaxed feeling come over me. That night I had the first good night's sleep in almost a year.

The next day I went to Emory Clinic for my doctor's report. He had all of the X rays in front of him, even the first ones from home where I had been in the hospital before. Each X ray showed a steady change and progression of what he termed as calcification of the pancreas, except in the last X ray. There on the last one, he could not find anything wrong at all. He was really shocked and could not explain his report.

At that time, I guess I was still in shock and did not realize this was really a miracle healing of God. I know now that this was God's power. To this day I have not had that pain again, and I praise Him!"

This past spring at school, I overheard conversation at a nearby lunch table—two classmates had made a profession-of-faith during last night's revival service, and had already planned to be baptized on the next Sunday evening. They had invited other friends to go to the evening's meeting—Miracles of Salvation.

Once several of our girls were late returning from break period. I found them seated in a large circle in the girls' rest room practicing for a seance. Soon they understood that the law does not allow cult or religious worship, as such, in the public schools. Our questions were answered in research. Laws of many kinds (including scriptural laws) were evaluated. These alert minds are searching. . . .

At no time do I instruct my students to worship sacred cows, to dance to a rainmaker's tune, to pray always facing the east, or the more factual to cast out demons. They are not being indoctrinated.

As their teacher, I ask that they always question everything that they hear, see and read, and to gain the habit of continually examining the facts—the results.

By need and habit, I find the time to meditate upon His Word. Students may see a Testament in my pocket book, and a Bible on my desk, for I have experienced that meditating in the Scriptures gives sustaining power beyond the flesh. "I will meditate in thy precepts, and have respect unto thy ways. I will delight myself in thy statutes: I will not forget thy word." (PSALM 119:15,16.)

The reason why I can write with such openness is that I live in the excitement of witnessing the Hand of God in my classroom. The Holy Spirit has been evident in my teaching labors. I am eternally thankful to our Lord that His promises are received and proven to be from His goodness and mercy.

Another teacher at our school who loves the Lord, observes with me the visible blessings of our Lord in even the insignificant details of our day-by-day adventures.

These students discern loving and empathizing understanding of their needs. And they respond to your honesty and caring. For 180 school days you'll chart their physical growth—some over 3 inches in 9 months. The mental and spiritual growth is immeasurable.

Two years ago, saintly Mr. R. O. Baker from Gideon International visited our classroom to graciously give testaments to any student who wanted one. Only one boy refused, as he stated that his dad was an atheist and he, himself, would not read it. No change in expression came on his face as Mr. Baker kindly said that he would leave other testaments on the teacher's desk if any new students would be enrolled. The red testaments were placed in the room closet, and classes continued on schedule. Before Christmas, this bright-minded young fellow quietly asked for a testament. After the holiday, I phoned the Gideon's listed number to have a message relayed to dear Mr. Baker. I was told that Mr. Baker observed this with the "great cloud of witnesses" for he had recently had his homegoing. Angels recorded the results. Grievously in some cases, these Bibles cannot be distributed because of another interpretation of the law.

Hundreds of teachers could write success stories of God's presence in the public school classroom.

The following quote is often found in publications: "The Constitution means what the Supreme Court says it means." We seem to be in a time when God has allowed the laws of our great nation to allow citizens to freely live their religious convictions in peace and prosperity.

Our news media can become so excited with the studies in mind-reach—precognition, and give full coverage on national television. Isn't it more spectacular—the miracles that physicians have documented? "Eye hath not seen, nor ear heard, neither have entered into the heart of man, the things which God hath prepared for them that love him." (I CORINTHIANS 2:9.)

When visiting in another state recently, I was surprised to hear an unusual criticism from an older churchman. He had heard that the charismatics in his denomination were really "loving it up" whenever they get together. He added that they embrace, smile, touch each other with greetings of "Praise the Lord." And then they hug, hold hands—great for fellowship, with singing and dancing and much "hallelujah." This surely grieved my heart, that anyone would keep his head buried in the sands of time, and not find himself in this great outpouring of God's mighty Spirit. It is the great Power of God's Spirit that overcomes the lustful flesh of man, and allows him to purely love his fellowman in holiness in the presence of his Heavenly Father.

"And it shall come to pass in the last days, saith God, I will pour out of my Spirit upon all flesh: and your sons and your daughters shall prophesy, and your young men shall see visions, and your old men shall dream dreams:

"And on my servants and on my handmaidens I will pour out in those days of my Spirit; and they shall prophesy: . . . And it shall come to pass, that whosoever shall call on the name of the Lord shall be saved." (ACTS 2:17,18,21.)

Once I heard this attention-getter at a State Education Association Meeting: "There are those educators who *make* things happen, and there are those educators who *watch* things happen. And then, there are those who wonder what happened."

To be truly educated, everyone should first *believe* that the Scripture is what it claims to be—the inspired Word of God. They should observe, *grow in* the fruits of the Holy Spirit, as they *experience* the gifts in the Spirit of God, and become more absorbed in the Living Word—the Living LORD JESUS CHRIST.

"And now I say unto you, Refrain from these men, and let them alone: for if this counsel or this work be of men, it will come to nought:

"But if it be of God, ye cannot overthrow it; lest haply ye be found even to fight against God." (ACTS 5:38,39.)

THIRTEEN

IF MY PEOPLE

"Submit yourselves to every ordinance of man for the Lord's sake: whether it be to the king, as supreme; Or unto governors, as unto them that are sent by him for the punishment of evildoers, and for the praise of them that do well.

For so is the will of God, that with well-doing ye may put to silence the ignorance of foolish men: As free, and not using your liberty for a cloak of maliciousness, but as the servants of God. Honour all men. Love the brotherhood. Fear God. Honour the king. . . . For this is thankworthy. . . ." (I PETER 2:13-19.)

Eleven- twelve-year-olds delight in memorizing the following thirty-five words from the Declaration of Independence:

We hold these truths to be self-evident, that all men are created equal, that they are endowed by their Creator with certain unalienable Rights, that among these are Life, Liberty and the pursuit of Happiness.

AMERICANISM TO BE TAUGHT: C. 49 provides for teaching Americanism in public schools. Americanism includes respect for law and order, respect for the national anthem and flag, duties of good citizenship, character and ideals of the founders of the country, a standard of good government and the constitution of the state and nation."*

---

*The North Carolina Law Review Vol. 1-19, 22-23, page 308. Chapel Hill: The School of Law by The University of North Carolina Press, 1923.

Permission to use the following has been granted by North Carolina Attorney General Rufus L. Edmisten, 29 March 1972

Subject: Education: Religion: Constitutional Law
Requested by: Honorable George Roundtree, III
Member of the North Carolina House of Representatives
Questions: (1) To what extent, if any, do the decisions of the United States Supreme Court permit programs of voluntary prayer to be instituted in the public schools of North Carolina?
(2) To what extent, if any, do the decisions of the United States Supreme Court permit voluntary programs of religious studies to be instituted in the public schools of North Carolina?
(3) May local boards of education provide for constitutionally permissible devotional periods and religious instruction without further legislative enactment?
Conclusions: (1) A moment of reverent silence is probably as much in the nature of a devotional program that may be instituted in the public schools.
(2) Religions may be studied in the public schools provided that the primary purpose and effect of any course of instruction in religion is to acquaint the student with knowledge of the religion being studied, rather than to inculcate in him any religious belief or disbelief.
(3) Yes, local boards of education have general supervisory powers to provide for constitutionally permissible devotional periods and courses of religious instruction.

The two leading United States Supreme Court cases in the area of devotional activities in the public schools are Engel v. Vitalie, 370 U.S. 421, 82 S. Ct. 1261, 8 L. Ed. 2d 601 (1962); and School District of Abington Township v. Schempp, 374 U.S. 203, 10 L. Ed. 2d 844, 83 S. Ct. 1506 (1963).
In "Engel" the following prayer was used to open the school day:

Almighty God, we acknowledge our dependence upon Thee, and we beg Thy blessings upon us, our parents, our teachers and our country.

The prayer required was nonsectarian. Students who objected to reciting it were allowed to be excused from the classroom. Despite the prayer's neutrality and its voluntary observance, the Supreme Court held that the devotional exercise by the public school was unconstitutional and in violation of the establishment clause of the First Amendment.

The "Schempp" case involved reading from the Bible and recitation of the Lord's Prayer. The Supreme Court found these devotional activities in the public schools also violative of the First Amendment and laid down the following test to determine whether or not devotions violated the First Amendment:

The test may be stated as follows:
What are the purposes and primary effect of the enactment? If either is the advancement or inhibition or religion, then the enactment exceeds the scope of legislative power as circumscribed by the Constitution. That is to say that to withstand the strictures of the Establishment Clause there must be a secular legislative purpose and a primary effect that neither advances nor inhibits religion. 374 U.S. at 222.

In a lengthy concurring opinion, Justice Brennan went on to suggest that "the observance of a moment of reverent silence at the opening of class" might adequately serve "the solely secular purposes" of the school devotional activities without jeopardizing either the religious liberties of any member of the community or the proper degree of separation between the spheres of religion and government. 374 U.S. 230.

Justice Brennan's suggestion that a moment of reverent silence is the most that can be done in the way of devotions in the public schools was borne out to be a decision of the United States Court of Appeals for the Seventh Circuit. In De Spain v. De Kalb Country Community School District, 384 F 2d 836

(7th Cir., 1967), the Court was faced with the following recitation by kindergarten children in a public school:

> We thank you for the flowers so sweet; we thank you for the food we eat; we thank you for the birds that sing; we thank you for everything.

The teacher argued that the primary purpose of the verse was secular; to teach the children gratitude and good manners. The Court held, however, that the verse constituted a prayer despite the fact that the word God was not used. Applying the Supreme Court's test of primary secular purpose and effect neither advancing nor inhibiting religion, the Court found that the primary purpose and effect of the verse in question was a religious act of praising and thanking the Deity. The recitation of the verse in question was, therefore, prohibited. If the Seventh Circuit has correctly interpreted the Supreme Court's decisions, and it appears to have done so, then Justice Brennan's suggestion that a moment of reverent silence is as much as can be done would seem to be correct.

One further point perhaps needs to be made. That is, of course, that the rules laid down by the Supreme Court apply to school authorities. School authorities may neither advance nor inhibit the cause of religion. School officials may no more compel Bible reading and prayer than they may prohibit individual students who wish to do so from praying or reading whatever religious materials they wish; provided, of course, that such activities on the part of students do not interfere with the operation of the schools.

The same basic rules that apply to prayer apply also to the teaching of religion in schools. It would appear to be perfectly proper to teach a course in religion provided that the primary purpose of the course was secular; that is, to acquaint the students with a knowledge of the religion under study rather than to inculcate in them any belief or disbelief. Thus, for example, a course of instruction in Christianity, Buddhism, and Islam would appear to be perfectly proper so long as the primary purpose and effect of the course was to study the beliefs of each of these religions, rather than to induce students to believe or disbelieve any of the beliefs studied.

It would appear that local boards of education presently have the power to institute constitutionally acceptable devotional periods and courses of instruction in religion as described above without further legislative enactment. "A moment of reverent silence" could be instituted under the general powers of a local school board as contained in G.S. 115-35 (b), " . . . Said boards of education shall have general control and supervision of all matters pertaining to the public schools and their respective administrative units. . . ." Under the same provision, local boards of education could provide for the teaching of religion as set out above, so long as the requirements of G.S. 115-37 (the teaching of courses prescribed by the State Superintendent of Public Instruction) are met.

ROBERT MORGAN, *Attorney General*
CHARLES A. LLOYD, *Associate Attorney*

FOURTEEN

FOR TEN'S SAKE

Our local Parent-Teacher Association at the school where I am teaching is all-inclusive in enlisting leadership. All members who will contribute ideas to help formulate the total year's schedule are sincerely welcomed. A school board attorney told me that PTA groups are not governed by the same laws that control the Public Schools. The Devotional Chairman thoughtfully considers the convictions of the entire community . . . in planning for this special part of each program. These moments of inspiration enhance the quality of these meetings. Here we can exercise our constitutional privileges as United States citizens who are concerned with the moral standards and values of our community. Living our belief is the test, the examination of our faith. It is this influence, this instilling of truths that captivate our young followers, that help to make their future more secure.

Research also shows that there can be no prohibition against teachers distributing religious tracts to other teachers.

The Wycliffe-JAARS Center at Waxhaw, North Carolina, graciously offers highlights for our social studies program. Their travelogue presentations are highly educational. The demonstrations of applying the art of linguistics to translate the Bible into any native language always presents a challenge. The study of the nature and structure of human speech is an active part of our interest. The Wycliffe interpreters usually are dressed in native costumes while displaying arts and crafts of the people who are being explored.

Our American National Red Cross chapter here in Charlotte has to be one of the best. Their commendable services to the entire community are widely recognized. Students from the full area are enlisted as their interests respond. Even public school teachers may receive credit for their teacher's certificate renewal. There are many accurate accounts here of young certified Basic First Aiders who bravely administered First Aid in emergency situations because of their excellent training from our Red Cross chapter.

The Salvation Army, YW/MCA, Little League, and other community groups help tremendously in character development among the youth in our area. The healthy competition and reception of trophies, and other awards, accent this outstanding contribution.

Also here, the universities and colleges offer tutoring service to students who wish to excel further in academic areas. These outstanding student-teacher programs have noticeably enriched this community.

Anyone is treading on delicate territory in trying to name all positive groups that have continually helped to advance our school endeavors. Personally I have observed and been a recipient of their dedicated labor in behalf of all of our school students:

The City-County Police and Fire Departments, The Cancer Society, the Lung, Heart, and Community Health Associations and all of the United Fund participants, the Boy and Girl Scouts of America; regular visits from the Duke Power Company and Southern Bell Telephone Company; the ready response of the Chamber of Commerce, *The Charlotte News* and *The Observer*; the full City of Charlotte, North Carolina, and all school-related organizations have to be among the top ten for a rating of excellence in providing for our youth.

During this past school year a simultaneous rebellion came from many students, parents, and teachers in several school districts against a false interpretation of Supreme Court ruling concerning the teaching of other theories of origins other than evolution. One such limited comment was that "Creation may have religious connotations that would bar teaching it in public schools."

Several parents, teachers, and an attorney appeared before a Board of Education meeting to request a change in the basic textbooks for eighth grade science and high school biology because of the conclusive statement for evolution. The State Text Book Commission has been contacted in regards to irregularities in a social studies textbook also. A group of parents and teachers have requested an appearance before the State Board of Education to have cleared other discrepancies if the following cannot be legally clarified in correspondence:

1. That all Theories of Origin (of the universe, earth, etc.) be explored in studies by our students.
2. That requirements not be made for students to keep their horoscopes, or take mini-courses in astrology, or accept as fact a time-line that man came from the ape-man branch by evolving from a one-cell arrangement.
3. That taxpayers' money not be funded for teacher-training courses in transcendental meditation.
4. That the legally permitted Moment of Meditation (State of North Carolina, Department of Justice—41 NCAG 802) be scheduled by all home room teachers for students—among whom will be some who desire to exercise their freedom of religion as provided by the law. When a teacher will not schedule the *permissive* Moment of Meditation—through what authority may students request their legal rights to exercise this privilege? Please refer to *When Free Men Shall Stand*, U.S. Senator Jesse Helms, A Zondervan Book, Chapter 21, "School Prayer."

Please review *Handy Dandy Evolution Refuter*, Robert E. Kofahl Ph.D., A Beta Book, Section J "How Old is the Earth?" Also, *The Theophilus Letters*, Don Ekerholm, Exposition, Press, chapters "Satanism" and "Teachings of the Devil."

We are caught up in an international verbal warfare among

scientists as explained by the Creation Research Society, based in Ann Arbor, Michigan, and the Creation-Science Research Center in San Diego, California.

"Oh let not the Lord be angry . . . and I will speak yet but this once; Peradventure ten shall be found there. And he said, I will not destroy it for ten's sake. And the Lord went his way . . ." (GENESIS 18:32.)

FIFTEEN

THE COUNSEL OF THE UNGODLY

"Blessed is the man that walketh not in the counsel of the ungodly, nor standeth in the way of sinners, nor sitteth in the seat of the scornful. . . .

The ungodly . . . are like the chaff which the wind driveth away.

Therefore the ungodly shall not stand in the judgment, nor sinners in the congregation of the righteous.

For the Lord knoweth the way of the righteous: but the way of the ungodly shall perish." (PSALMS 1:1-6.)

Another active spiritual law is: The judgment in which we judge, judges us in return. (MATTHEW 7:1.)

"And ye shall know the truth, and the truth shall make you free." (JOHN 8:32.)

"Then Jesus sent the multitude away, and went into the house: and his disciples came unto him, saying, Declare unto us the parable of the tares of the field.

"He answered and said unto them, He that soweth the good seed is the Son of man; The field is the world; the good seed are the children of the kingdom; but the tares are the children of the wicked one; The enemy that sowed them is the devil; the harvest is the end of the world; and the reapers are the angels.

"As therefore the tares are gathered and burned in the fire; so shall it be in the end of this world.

The Counsel of the Ungodly

"The Son of man shall send forth his angels, and they shall gather out of his kingdom all things that offend, and them which do iniquity; And shall cast them into a furnace of fire: there shall be wailing and gnashing of teeth.

"Then shall the righteous shine forth as the sun in the kingdom of their Father. Who hath ears to hear, let him hear." (MATTHEW 13:36-43.)

Irreligious teachers, parents, and school administrators will answer to their Creator in this life as well.

A thorough or even a slight study of the history of any nation will prove that " . . . where there is no vision, the people perish: but he that keepeth the law, happy is he." (PROVERBS 29:18.)

Without fail, wherever individual, group, or national moral and spiritual values break away from God's heaven-bound standards spiritual poverty and destruction follow. Without exception, history declares the repeated failures of mankind.

Since some minority groups have established a pattern of rebutting the constitutional freedoms of men with their negative philosophy, a greeting can await in print. Unnumbered prayers are around the throne of our Heavenly Father for the salvation of all of those whose consciences have become seared. Why don't they scientifically analyze the deathbed scene of atheists and other rejectors. Their obvious fears and anguishes are only a glimpse into the Hell prepared for Satan and his legions.

This intent investigation of results-conclusions could bring the despairing under God's convicting power of a new birth experience. " . . . His goodness and mercy endureth forever."

Everyone should investigate the brilliant study of God's miracles in *The Truth about Miracles* by H. Richard Casdorph, MD.PhD. Here he scientifically reviews recent histories of miraculous healings. Proof of healings are verified with medical records and testimonies.

" . . . Prove me, now herewith, saith the Lord of hosts, if I will not open you the windows of heaven, and pour you out a blessing, that there shall not be room enough to receive it." (MALACHI 3:10.)

"For we wrestle not against flesh and blood, but against principalities, against powers, against the rulers of the darkness of this world, against spiritual wickedness in high places." (EPHESIANS 6:12.)

Jesus had much to say about Satan. He called him "the enemy, the evil one, the prince of this world; A liar, the father of lies; a murderer; the tempter." Jesus said that he "saw him fallen from heaven." Satan has a "kingdom," and "evil men are his sons." Satan "snatches the Word from hearers," and he "bound a woman for eighteen years." He "desired to have Peter." Satan has "angels" and " . . . eternal fire is prepared for him."

Twelve-year-olds begin to more clearly understand our citizenship privileges that are based on the four constitutional freedoms—the essential human freedoms: Freedom of Speech, Freedom of Worship, Freedom from Want, Freedom from Fear.

Along with the knowledge in understanding will come wisdom, when our students begin to comprehend the freedoms of God to man: God created us with the freedom to think. The choices that we make—positive or negative—are made with the freedom of conscience.

"Choose you this day whom ye will serve." (JOSHUA 24:15.)

"Being then made free from sin, ye became the servants of righteousness." (ROMANS 6:18.)

"As free, and not using your liberty for a cloak of maliciousness, but as the servants of God." (I PETER 2:16.)

" . . . let me freely speak unto you. . . ." (ACTS 2:29.)

" . . . And let him that is athirst, Come. And whosoever will, let him take the water of life freely." (REVELATIONS 22:17.)

The miracles in Jesus' days on earth were so numerous and publicized that the sinners and Pharisees acknowledged that these were miracles. But because of the hardness of their hearts, they attributed them to Satanic powers. Educators need to take heed.

"Wherefore I say unto you, All manner of sin and blasphemy shall be forgiven unto men: but the blasphemy against the Holy Ghost shall not be forgiven unto men.

The Counsel of the Ungodly

"And whosoever speaketh a word against the Son of man, it shall be forgiven him: but whosoever speaketh against the Holy Ghost, it shall not be forgiven him, neither in this world, neither in the world to come.

"But I say unto you, that every idle word that men shall speak, they shall give account thereof in the day of judgment. For by thy words thou shalt be justified, and by thy words thou shall be condemned." (MATTHEW 12:31,32,36.)

SIXTEEN

RIVERS OF LIVING WATER

" . . . and it was a river that I could not pass over: for the waters were risen, waters to swim in, a river that could not be passed over. . . . And it shall come to pass, that everything that liveth, which moveth, whithersoever the rivers shall come, shall live: . . . for they shall be healed:" (EZEKIEL 47:5,9.)

This climactic chapter is to project an alarm, a catalyst for all Christian educators to stay in the mainstream of God's great abundance, by constantly exercising His governing currents, His basic principles of communing with Him as we communicate with each other . . . always in the flow of His loving Power.

Our Lord God, having unlimited power, being present everywhere and having total knowledge is not governed by man's law.

> Blessed is he that READETH, and they that HEAR the words of this prophecy and KEEP those things which are written therein: for the time IS at hand. (REVELATION 1:3.)

Years ago a beloved Sunday school teacher expounded these truths which I marked in my Bible: Formulas from God, Psalm 37, David's philosophy amidst the sinful confusion of his day.

> TRUST in the Lord and DO GOOD=Thou shalt be fed.
> DELIGHT thyself also in the Lord=and He shall give thee the desires of thine heart.
> COMMIT thy way unto the Lord=and He shall bring it

Rivers of Living Water

to pass. REST in the Lord, WAIT patiently for Him, FRET NOT, CEASE from anger, FORSAKE wrath=for evildoers shall be cut off. Those that WAIT upon the Lord=They shall INHERIT the earth.

All devoted Bible teachers will understand God's methods of guiding us in His Will under His commandments:

1. *God's Word* Blessed are they that hear the word of God, and keep it. (LUKE 11:28.)
2. *Holy Spirit* The Holy Ghost teacheth; comparing spiritual things with spiritual. (I CORINTHIANS 2:13.)
3. *Counsel* Every purpose is established by counsel. (PROVERBS 20:18.)
4. *Circumstance* And we know that all things work together for good to them that love God, to them who are the called according to his purpose. (ROMANS 8:28.)

Christian implications of educational principles are unlimited. As all diligent educators must agree, the basic educational concepts are within the framework of Biblical teachings. To hear a Christian psychiatrist expound these exciting truths is to become grounded in the eternal love of our Creator. "For God hath not given us the spirit of fear; but of power, and of love, and of a sound mind." (II TIMOTHY 1:7.)

Now you may be wondering about the practical application of all of this elevated wordage to the individual classroom situation. That's the purpose of this manuscript,—to prove to you, the reader, that time and experience have proven to me, a student/teacher, that God's power is evident, is obviously active in my personal involvement with students, parents, teachers, and all administrators, for He is with everyone who will "call upon Him . . . according to His purpose . . . to supply our needs." "He that believeth on me, as the scripture hath said, out of his heart shall flow rivers of living water." (JOHN 7:38.)

Every classroom situation has scriptural connotations. Our Lord God who created all knowledge with which we may use

His wisdom to apply, according to methods which he projected in creation, is actively permeated within the entire school program. He has ordained the educational system.

In the 1800s, saintly Horatio G. Spafford and Philip P. Bliss captured the heart of the gospel message in their blessed hymn of assurance, "It Is Well with My Soul:"

> When peace, like a river, attendeth my way,
> When sorrows like sea billows roll;
> Whatever my lot, Thou hast taught me to say,
> It is well, it is well with my soul.
>
> And, Lord haste the day when the faith shall be sight,
> The clouds be roll'd back as a scroll,
> The trump shall resound and the Lord shall descend,
> "Even so," it is well with my soul.

Kinley Library
Columbia College
8th and Rogers
Columbia, MO. 65201